P9-AOF-741

# BECOMING AMERICAN

# BECOMING AMERICAN

# AMERICAN

*The African-American Journey*

## HOWARD DODSON

*Director, Schomburg Center for Research
in Black Culture, New York Public Library*

WITH

## CHRISTOPHER MOORE &
## ROBERTA YANCY

STERLING

New York / London
**www.sterlingpublishing.com**

STERLING and the distinctive Sterling logo are registered trademarks of
Sterling Publishing Co., Inc.

**Library of Congress Cataloging in Publication Data**

Dodson, Howard.
  Becoming American : the African-American journey / Howard Dodson ; with Christopher
Moore & Roberta Yancy.
      p. cm.
  Includes bibliographical references.
  ISBN 978-1-4027-5407-4
  1. African Americans--History. 2. African Americans--History--Sources. 3. African
Americans--Ethnic identity. 4. African diaspora. I. Moore, Christopher Paul, 1952- II. Yancy,
Roberta. III. Title.

  E185.D623 2009
  973'.0496073--dc22

                             2008036171

                    2  4  6  8  10  9  7  5  3  1

                 Published by Sterling Publishing Co., Inc.
                387 Park Avenue South, New York, NY 10016
                        © 2009 by Howard Dodson

         *Please see picture credits page for image credits and permissions.*

                 Distributed in Canada by Sterling Publishing
                  ℅ Canadian Manda Group, 165 Dufferin Street
                       Toronto, Ontario, Canada M6K 3H6
             Distributed in the United Kingdom by GMC Distribution Services
           Castle Place, 166 High Street, Lewes, East Sussex, England BN7 1XU
               Distributed in Australia by Capricorn Link (Australia) Pty. Ltd.
                      P.O. Box 704, Windsor, NSW 2756, Australia

                      Sterling ISBN 978-1-4027-5407-4

            For information about custom editions, special sales, premium and
                corporate purchases, please contact Sterling Special Sales
         Department at 800-805-5489 or specialsales@sterlingpublishing.com.

*Frontispiece:* On July 28, 1917, approximately 8,000 black Americans silently marched
down Fifth Avenue in New York City in the Silent March, organized by Harlem religious and civic leaders and the NAACP as a protest against lynching, violence, and
racial discrimination.

# CONTENTS

# INTRODUCTION

# Becoming American:
# The African-American Journey

I majored in social studies and history in undergraduate school and at the masters level. Nevertheless, I was well into the second year of my masters program before I had an opportunity to take my first course dealing with black people. It was a course in African politics offered in the early 1960s as Africa was just beginning to break the bonds of colonialism. I had gone through grade school, junior and senior high, undergraduate school, and a year of graduate school before any aspect of the black experience was offered as a formal part of the curriculum. What I had learned prior to that was what a few conscientious black teachers in the all-black grade school and junior high school in Chester, Pennsylvania, slipped into their courses. Mostly, they taught about black heroes and sheroes like Frederick Douglass, Sojourner Truth, Harriett Tubman, Booker T. Washington, and George Washington Carver—black role models to be emulated. Black history was essentially black biography—hero and shero stories about great black men and women who triumphed over the odds.

Not until I enrolled in the Ph.D. program in black history at the University of California at Berkeley in 1970 did I begin to see the breadth, depth, and impact of the black experience not only in the United States but throughout the world. Almost everywhere one looked in America, the impact of black peoples' presence, creativity, laboring activity, and social and cultural imprint was there for all to see. But few saw it and even fewer had studied it. Only a very few had studied as much as I. Over the last thirty-five years or more, I have spent my life learning all I could about the black experience and making that knowledge available to the public—children and adults, blacks and whites, and all the rest of humankind. This book,

Detail of a c. 1874 lithograph depicting South Carolina representative Robert B. Elliott delivering his famous speech in favor of the Civil Rights Act to the House of Representatives, January 6, 1874.

*Becoming American: The African-American Journey,* is a chronological history of African Americans as it has evolved within the context of American and world history.

The African-American experience in the United States had its origins on the continent of Africa. Indeed, all of humankind traces its roots back to Africa. Whether one uses the biblical Adam and Eve or the anthropological Lucy as a point of origin, Africa is recognized as the place where human beings originated as a species. Ancient Egypt, the most highly developed ancient civilization, called itself Kemet, which means "Land of the Blacks." Nevertheless, well into the twentieth century it was widely believed in the Western world that black people had no history or culture. Twentieth-century scholarship has largely refuted these myths, but Americans have not been introduced to the facts.

Indeed, most Americans—including far too many Americans of African descent—have little or no knowledge of the central role that people of African descent have played in the making of history both here in the United States and throughout the western hemisphere. Even less is known about the presence and role of African peoples in the history of all humankind. And except for an occasional televised documentary film or serious movie on black themes, the majority of American people have had few opportunities to discover the richness and diversity of the black experience in America or compare it with the black experience in other parts of the world.

Too often, the telling of the story of African Americans begins with the transatlantic slave trade, and the whole of our history has too frequently been organized around our victimization during the eras of slavery and racial segregation. The triumphs of the civil rights movement, especially the role of Martin Luther King Jr., are chronicled, as are the recent challenges facing blacks in urban America. The centrality of blacks' self-initiated activities in the making of African-American history is not always apparent, and their active role over the last two hundred plus years in defining and redefining the very concept of America and Americans is usually not fully appreciated.

*Becoming American: The African-American Journey* offers a unique chrono-logical approach that affords readers an opportunity to begin discovering the active, generative role blacks have played in the making of America as we know it today. It also reveals the ways in which blacks' attempts to make America live up to its founding creed have kept them on the path to "Becoming American."

Chronologies like timelines are useful devices for locating specific people, events, and activities in their proper contexts. African-American history, which traces its roots back to Africa, has unfolded within the context of the formation, development, and underdevelopment of the American (USA) nation-state as well as the broader African and global world. While there is not always a causal relationship among events, people, and activities, there are frequently associational ones. Events in Europe, Africa, and the Caribbean, for instance, frequently resonate with, if not draw some inspiration from, events and movements in the United States. And vice versa. The anticolonial struggles in Africa during the 1950s and 1960s inspired the civil rights movement in the United States. And the civil rights movement was a catalyst for the antiapartheid struggle in South Africa.

Of equal significance, the victories won by African Americans in their civil and human rights struggles encouraged the development of the women's and gay rights movements among others. Reading *Becoming American* helps us see and understand the ways in which the African-American experience relates to and at times interacts with things that are happening in the United States and the wider world.

The African-American journey to becoming American is not simply a chronicling of black involvement in the major events of what we have come to know as American history. Rather, *Becoming American* is a chronicle of black Americans' day-to-day wrestling with the contradictions between America's ideals of freedom, justice, and equality and the constant, blatant violation of those ideals and principles vis-à-vis black people. African Americans' firm belief in America—our unwavering faith in its founding ideals and principles—is what has kept us struggling for full rights as Americans, even as the nation's policies and practices frustrated our ambitions and challenged our faith. African Americans' insistence on enjoying the rights promised by the nation's founding creed has, in turn, constantly challenged America to live up to its ideals and principles and make their imagined, idealized America real.

*Becoming American: The African-American Journey* is designed to offer readers a brief introduction to some seminal moments, events, and personalities in African-American history as well as to major documents and voices that have defined and shaped the black historical, political, social, and cultural presence on the American landscape.

This book is organized into two sections. In Part One, we present a chronology of major events in African-American history, compared with major events in world history, with emphasis on African and African diasporan history. Quotes from major historic documents and figures are interspersed throughout and linked to critical moments in the chronology. Longer selections from historic documents that have shaped the African-American experience, as well as critical documents in African Americans' own words, make up Part Two of the book, providing further evidence of the role of black people in American and world history.

This brief survey is not meant to be exhaustive in any way. Rather, its purpose is to lead and encourage readers to explore these events and personalities in greater depth. *Becoming American: The African-American Journey* is your passport to the extraordinary African-American presence in American and world history.

—*Howard Dodson, Director,*
*Schomburg Center for Research in Black Culture*

# PART ONE

## Timeline of
## African-American &
## Global/African Diasporan History

**4–2.7 million years** BCE Hominid species *Australopithicus afarensis* lives in Hadar region of Ethiopia, including "Lucy" (skeletal remains found in 1974)

**c. 1.5 million years** BCE *Homo erectus* leaves Africa to populate other parts of world

**200,000–100,000** BCE *Homo sapiens* spread nomadically throughout Africa and other continents

**50,000–100** BCE Rock paintings made in North, Central, and South Africa; among oldest are those produced by the Khoikhoi in Namibia

**8000** BCE In Niger, Kiffian culture thrives in era of "Green Sahara," producing pottery and ivory ornaments

**6000–4000** BCE Agriculture spreads throughout Africa

**4500–1000** BCE Ancient African civilizations flourish in Nile Valley, at Egypt and Nubia

**c. 3200** BCE Egyptian writing (hieroglyphics) invented

**c. 2780–2750** BCE Step Pyramid of King Djoser by Egyptian architect Imhotep

**c. 2560–2540** BCE Great Pyramid of Khufu (Cheops) built over 20-year period in Giza (present-day greater Cairo); only surviving monument of original Seven Ancient Wonders of the World

**2000–1000** BCE Bantu migrate across equatorial sub-Saharan Africa

**1730–1580** BCE African Kingdom of Kush controls Nubia south of Elephantine Island

**1400–600** BCE Iron smelting in west, east, and south Africa

**1000** BCE–**350** BCE Kingdom of Nubia flourishes

**c. 900** BCE–**200** BCE Nok civilization and culture thrive in Nigeria

**160** BCE Terence Afer (the African) considered Roman Empire's finest Latin translator and poet:

> *"Homo sum: humani nihil a me alienum puto.* (I am a man; I think nothing human is alien to me.)"
> —TERENCE, *Heauton Timorunmenos*, 163 BCE

**c. 50** BCE Fifteen thousand Gallic (modern France, Belgium, and western Germany) slaves begin to arrive in Rome per year, for several years, in exchange for Italian wine

**c. 50** BCE–**476** CE Slavery fuels Roman Empire for several hundred years; 2 million slaves from Europe, Middle East, and Africa, estimated in Italy at end of Republic

**c. 50** BCE–**700** CE Aksum Kingdom flourishes in Ethiopia

**c. 4** BCE Birth of Jesus

**c. 320** CE Christianization of Ethiopia begins

**c. 400–1076** African Kingdom of Ghana flourishes in West Africa

*420* Christian theologian Augustine of Hippo in North Africa stresses equality of all humans

*c. 500–1400* Middle Ages: Slave trade of Slavs, and whites from all over Europe, and to lesser extent, Africans, flourishes throughout Europe

*c. 550–1000* Celts, Franks, Goths, Visogoths, and Anglo-Saxons commonly provide slaves to winning armies

*608–916* During Tang Dynasty, China engages in sea trade with African merchants

*649* Balthild, an Anglo-Saxon slave, marries King Clovis II; later made Saint Balthild for her personal campaign to stop slave trade and end slavery

*c. 750* Islam introduced to West Africa

*800–1400* Battling Muslim and Christian armies on land and sea commonly seize and enslave one another

*987* Founded in third century BCE, Paris made capital of France

*c. 1000* Slavery declines in northern and central Europe. Slaves converted into serfs, bonded laborers provided with houses, and they work fields for manor lords in return for protection

*c. 1000* From Nok, Yoruba and Benin cultures emerge

*1000* Shona (House of Stone) empire of Zimbabwe emerges

*1068* A trader to Senegambia (present-day Senegal and Gambia) observes much cultivation of cotton: "Every house had its cotton bush" and "cloths of fine cotton"

*c. 1200* Slavery ends in England, but continues in Ireland. Slavery continues in countries that border Mediterranean

*c. 1200* Lalibela, King of Ethiopia, creates ceremonial center of 11 churches carved in stone in Roha (now known as Lalibela)

*c. 1200* Aztec Empire develops in Central America

*1200–1300* In 13th century, royal buyers in Nice, Arles, Venice, Sicily, and Genoa are among the main purchasers of African slaves

*1235* Empire of Mali founded in West Africa by Sundiata Keita

*c. 1260* Timbuktu emerges as political, academic, commercial, and religious center of Mali Empire

*1260* Spanish slavery code, approved by Vatican, keeps married couples from being separated, provides legal protection against mistreatment, and allows slaves to inherit property

*1300* Kingdom of Benin emerges in West Africa

*1324* King Mansa Musa of Mali makes Mecca pilgrimage

*1350* Drastic population decline in Europe due to Black Death causes acute labor shortages, which economically encourages free peasants over serfdom and slaves

*1358* Rise of Ngola Dynasty in West Africa

*1390* King of Bornu (in Nigeria) complains to sultan of Egypt that Arabs are always seizing "our people as merchandise"

*1400* Africans in Christian religious iconography proliferate in Europe, including Balthazar (the black wise man) and Saints Maurice and Gregory

*1415* Portugal's Henry the Navigator encourages exploration of African coast

*1418* Portuguese land on Madeira Islands; they later plant sugarcane from Sicily

*c. 1420* European visitors report thriving copper and iron industry in Senegambia, with steel production comparable to Europe; a traveler notes extraordinary fineness that West African craftsmen achieve with metal

*1421* Chinese ships believed to visit North and South America

*1441* Portuguese trade for gold and kidnap 12 Africans from Cabo Blanco and enslave them in Portugal

*1442–44* Portuguese stage raids for slaves, who often kill their attackers

*1445* On coast of Senegal, Portuguese begin to buy slaves, though kidnapping continues

*1445* Portuguese ships transport about 200 slaves annually to Lisbon, Seville, Portuguese islands in the Azores, and Madeira

*1446* Portuguese establish trading post along West African coast

*c. 1450* Gutenberg uses metal plates for printing

*1450–60* About 1,000 slaves annually transported to Europe

*1450–1550* Before shipment to the Americas, many slaves sent first to Portugal, Spain, Italy, and Sicily for "Christianization"

*1453* Ottoman Turks capture Constantinople and divert trade in European slaves to Islamic market

*1455* Venetian navigator Alvise Ca' da Mosto explores Senegal River

*1456* Ca' da Mosto sails up Gambia River 60 miles, to trade for slaves; reaches Cape Verde Islands

*1459* Debate in Venetian senate expresses need for more African slaves

*1460* Sultan of Bengal acquires 500 African slaves, purchases more annually

*1462* Papal bull by Pope Pius II forbids enslavement of recently converted Africans

*1464* Empire of Songhai arises in West Africa

*1468* Songhai king Sunni Ali captures Timbuktu

*1470* Portuguese navigators discover Gold Coast, West Africa

*1474* Ferdinand and Isabella create office of Mayor of the Africans in Seville

*1476* Spain occupies Canary Islands

*1477* Spanish soldiers end slave revolt on Canary Islands

*1480* Portuguese market slaves to vineyards and small sugar plantations in Italy and Sicily

*1480* German artist Erasmus Grasser creates sculptures based on Moorish dancers who toured European courts.

*1482* Portuguese build first slave trading fort at Elmina, Gold Coast

*1484* Portuguese navigator Diego Cam enters mouth of Congo River

*1486* Kingdom of Benin begins to trade slaves for European guns and other goods

*1486* African slaves rebel in Bengal, India, and install their own leader, Firuz Shah, as sultan (1487–90)

*c. 1490* Enslaved Africans shipped to Barcelona and Valencia at rate of 250 per year

*1492* Spanish conquer Granada, ending Moor rule; Moors and Jews expelled from Iberian Peninsula

*1492* Christopher Columbus sails from Spain, landing in Bahamas, Cuba, and Haiti; black navigator Pedro Alonso Niño travels with him

*1493* Columbus lands at Puerto Rico, Dominica; he lands at Jamaica following year

*1493* Romano Pane, monk accompanying Columbus, describes tobacco plant

*1494* Pope Alexander VI issues Treaty of Tordesillas, dividing New World between Spain and Portugal

*1496* Jews expelled from Portugal; many will settle in Brazil and the Caribbean

*1498* Six hundred Caribs from West Indies enslaved and shipped to Spain

*1499–1502* Italian navigator Amerigo Vespucci explores east coast of South America

*1500* Pope Alexander VI celebrates discovery of New World, proclaims "Year of Jubilee"

*1500* Pedro Álvares Cabral discovers Brazil, claiming it for Portugal

*1501* Portuguese explorers discover *pau brasil* (brazil wood tree) from which natives create red dye

*1502* Columbus sails, on his fourth and final voyage, to Honduras and Panama; Queen Isabella authorizes slaves "born in the power of Christians" to "pass to" the West Indies

*1503* Zanzibar becomes Portuguese colony

*1505* Seventeen enslaved Africans sent from Seville to Hispaniola

*1506* Baptism of Nzinga Mbemba, who becomes Afonso I, first Catholic King of the Kongo (Congo / Angola)

*1507* German cartographer Martin Waldseemüller publishes first map with the name America (after Amerigo Vespucci) for the New World

*1507* Ca' da Mosto's *La Prima Navigazione per l'Oceano alle terre de' Negri della Bassa Ethiopia (The First Ocean Voyage to the Land of the Blacks in Lower Ethiopia)*, about exploration of Gambia, published posthumously in Venice

*1511* Diego de Velásquez de Cuéllar conquers natives in Cuba

*1511* Enslaved Africans sent to cultivate Cuba for European settlement

*1512* Due to disease and warfare, some 200,000 Native Americans died in 20 years following European arrival

*1513* Juan Ponce de León explores North American east coast from Florida to Carolinas for Spain

*1513* Traveling with 30 persons of African descent, Spain's Balboa crosses Middle America and sights Pacific Ocean

*1514* King Ferdinand restricts importation of slaves into Spain, fearing growing black population a security risk

*1516* Indigo (dye) from the Americas first exported to Europe

*1516* First sugar mill in Western Hemisphere constructed in Hispaniola (Dominican Republic)

*1517* Bartolomé de Las Casas proposes each Spanish settler bring 12 slaves to New World

*1517* Martin Luther questions infallibility of papal decisions, sparks Protestant Reformation in Europe

*1518* Eighteen-year-old Archduke Charles, later Emperor Charles V, grants monopoly of slave trade to a Flemish merchant

*1518* License to import 4,000 African slaves to Spanish colonies granted to Lorens de Gominot of Spain; license lessens practice of first bringing slaves to Europe before sending them on to the Americas

*1518* First slaves shipped directly from Guinea Coast to West Indies, bypassing stay in Spain and making trade more profitable

*1519* Hernán Cortés leads Spanish conquest of Aztecs in Mexico, accompanied by six Africans who grow America's first wheat crop

*1520* Spanish ships leave Mexico carrying gold and silver looted from Aztecs

*1520* Cocoa exported from Mexico to Spain

*1520* *Marriage of St. Ursula to Prince Conan*, painting in a Lisbon monastery, depicts several African musicians performing for royalty

*1521* Cortés takes control of Mexico after defeating Aztecs

*1522* African slaves stage an uprising in Hispaniola

*1523* African slaves and soldiers accompany Don Pedro de Alvarado into Guatemala

*1524* Giovanni da Verrazzano discovers New York Bay

*1524* Spanish conqueror Francisco Pizarro enters Ecuador and Peru; free and enslaved Africans among his crew, serving as sailors, soldiers, and laborers

*1524* Turkeys from South America eaten for first time at English court

## AFRICANS IN COLONIAL AMERICA

*1525* Black Portuguese navigator Esteban Gómez sails into bay discovered by Italian explorer Giovanni da Verrazzano previous year, and later renamed the Hudson River after English explorer Henry Hudson who arrived in 1609

*1526* First enslaved Africans in continental North America arrive in South Carolina/Georgia region; within a few months they run away

*1525* Spanish infantry begins to use muskets

*1526* Kongo King Afonso I sends formal protest to Portugal regarding devastation caused by slave trade

*1526* Portuguese vessels arrive in New Guinea

*1527* Slave insurrections in Puerto Rico and Mexico City, where there are rumors that Africans have chosen king to take over country

*1528* Augsburg merchants receive from Charles V right to colonize Venezuela

*1529* Slaves set fire to Santa Marta, capital of Magdalena, Columbia

*1530* Practice of Christianizing slaves in Europe ending, with large enslaved and free populations remaining in Lisbon, Seville, Granada, and Sicily

*1530* Pope Clement VII crowns Charles V Holy Roman Emperor

**1530** Portuguese colonize Brazil

**1531** Henry VIII recognized as Supreme Head of Church of England

**1531** University of Granada founded in Spain

**1532** Estebán, Moroccan-born Muslim slave of Spaniard Andrés Dorantes, explores southwestern US with Dorantes and two other survivors of 1527 Pánfilo de Narváez expedition to Florida

**1532** Sugarcane first cultivated in Brazil

**1533** Pizarro defeats Inca of Peru and plunders native cities; ships returning to Europe laden with gold and silver are envy of Europe

**1534** Estebán escapes after capture by local Indians and with three Spaniards, including explorer Álvar Núñez Cabeza de Vaca, crosses through lower Gulf Coast region of US to Upper Mexico, reaching Mexico City in 1536

**1534** Jacques Cartier makes first visit to North America, sights coast of Labrador

**1535** Charles V conquers Tunis, frees 20,000 Christian slaves

**1535** Enslaved Africans clear land and build roads for Spanish settlements in Peru

**1536** John Calvin publishes his influential *Institutes of the Christian Religion*, leads second Protestant Reformation in France

**1536** With slave labor, Spaniard Pedro de Mendoza founds Buenos Aires, Argentina

**1536** Enslaved Africans and free blacks, mainly soldiers, sailors, and craftsmen from Seville, arrive in Puerto Rico

**1537** Pope Paul III declares that indigenous peoples of the Americas are not to be enslaved

**1537** Alessandro de Medici, son of a black mother and a father believed to have been Pope Clement VII, assassinated by rival cousin

**1538** Mapmakers use name *America* for both northern and southern continents for first time

**1538** First Africans arrive in Bahia, Brazil

**1538** With slave labor, Bogotá, Colombia, is founded by Gonzalo Jiménez de Quesada

*1539–42* Hernando de Soto explores southeastern United States

*1539* De Soto explores Florida, accompanied by African slaves

*1541* Francisco de Coronado explores Arizona, New Mexico, Texas, Oklahoma, and Kansas, accompanied by African slaves

*1541* De Soto discovers Mississippi River

*1542* Juan Rodríguez Cabrillo explores California coast

*1542* Spanish crown outlaws enslavement of Native Americans, resulting in intensification of African slave trade

*1540* Juan Valiente, former slave and Indian fighter, receives large estate near Santiago, Chile, as reward for fighting Incas

*1542* Thirty thousand Africans in Hispaniola, with 10 percent living in *Cimarrón* (Maroon) colonies (in Spanish, *cimarrón* means "runaway slave")

*1543* Spanish royal decree in West Indies prohibits enslavement of Muslims who have converted to Christianity

*1543* Discovery of silver mines of Potosí, Peru

*1545* First Roman Catholic Council of Trent session establishes doctrine in response to Protestant Reformation, emphasizing differences between Catholics and Protestants

*1548* Guinea pepper plant grown in England

*1548* Silver mines of Zacatecas, Mexico, mined by enslaved Africans

*c. 1548* Free and enslaved black artisans in Peru manufacture swords, lances, and rosaries for Spanish army

*1549* Father Manuel de Nóbrega arrives in Bahia from Lisbon, protests enslavement of Africans

*1549* With slave labor, Tomé de Souza founds São Salvador, Brazil

*1550* Slave insurrections in Peru and Nicaragua

| AFRICAN-AMERICAN | GLOBAL / AFRICAN DIASPORAN |
|---|---|
| | *1551* University of San Marcos founded in Lima, Peru; oldest university in the Americas |
| | *1551* Ottoman Turks capture Tripoli, Libya |
| | *1552* Slave insurrections in Panama and Venezuela |
| | *1553* Pedro de Cieza de León describes potato in his *Chronicle of Peru* |
| | *1553* *Cimarrón* (Maroon) colony arises in Panama |
| *1555* Dominican priest Fernão de Oliveira publishes his treatise *Arte da guerra do mar* (*Art of War at Sea*), condemning slavery: | *1555* With help of slave labor, short-lived French Huguenot colony of France Antarctique founded on island in Rio de Janeiro Bay (Guanabara Bay) |

"It is no excuse to say that they sell one another, for he who buys what is badly sold is still guilty . . . because if there were no buyers, there would be no bad sellers, nor thieves to steal for sale."

| AFRICAN-AMERICAN | GLOBAL / AFRICAN DIASPORAN |
|---|---|
| | *1556* Charles V abdicates, assigning Spain to his son Philip and Holy Roman Empire to his brother Ferdinand I |
| | *1557* State bankruptcy in France and Spain |
| | *1559* Coronation of Queen Elizabeth I in England |
| | *1560* Jean Nicot de Villemain, France's ambassador to Portugal, writes of tobacco's medicinal properties, describing it as cure-all |
| | *1560* On Hispaniola, Africans outnumber Europeans 15 to 1 |
| *1562* French Huguenots establish short-lived colony at Port Royal, South Carolina | *1562* First English slaving expedition by Sir John Hawkins from Guinea to West Indies |
| | *c. 1563* Term "Puritan" first used in England |
| | *1563* Outbreak of plague in Europe; over 20,000 die in London |

| AFRICAN-AMERICAN | GLOBAL/AFRICAN DIASPORAN |
|---|---|
| *1564* French attempt to colonize Florida at Fort Caroline (present-day Jacksonville, Florida) | *1564* Queen Elizabeth I funds second slave-trading expedition by Sir John Hawkins, who illegally sells slaves to Spanish planters in West Indies |
| *1564* English navigator Sir John Hawkins, pioneer of English slave trade and cousin of Francis Drake, sells 400 African slaves in the West Indies and visits French colony in Florida | |
| *1565* African artisans and farmers accompany Spanish settlement of San Agustín (St. Augustine, Florida) | *1565* Sweet potatoes and tobacco introduced in England |
| | *1565* Juan Latino, Afro-Spanish scholar, made grammar chairman at Cathedral School of Granada |
| | *1565* Rio de Janeiro, Brazil, founded by Portuguese with aid of slave labor |
| *1566* First Jesuits arrive in Florida | *1566* East Africa claimed as Portuguese territory |
| | *c. 1568* Spanish trade route between Mexico and the Philippines introduces enslaved Africans to the Philippines |
| | *1568* Treaty of Longjumeau ends War of Religion in France |
| | *1569* Morisco Rebellion, revolt against forced Muslim-to-Christian conversions, suppressed in Granada |
| | *1560* Rebel leader Bayano founds Maroon colony in Ronconcholon in eastern Panama |
| | *1570* Panamanian Maroons found town of Santiago del Principe |
| *1572* Jesuits withdraw from Florida, over next few years Franciscans take their place | *1572* Francis Drake attacks Spanish harbors in America |
| *1573–85* Juan Latino publishes three books of poetry; one of them in form of an address to King Philip of Spain: | *1573* Construction, with slave labor, begins on Metropolitan Cathedral of Mexico City (finished in 1813) |

"If our black face, oh king, is displeasing to your ministers, the white face is not pleasing to the men of Ethiopia."

*1573* First German sugarcane refinery opens in Augsburg

*1574* Portuguese colonize Angola, found São Paulo harbor

*1575* More than 50,000 slaves exported from Angola to Brazil between 1575 and 1591

*1575* State bankruptcy in Spain

*1576* African soldiers destroy Portuguese fort at Accra (Ghana)

*1577* Richard Eden publishes *History of Travel in West and East Indies*

*1577* Viceroy of Peru bans slaves from owning weapons; nominally "free blacks" ordered to take residence with Spanish masters

*1578* In Sicily, miraculous acts associated with Friar Benedict the Moor, son of enslaved Africans; he is called *Il Moro Santo* (The Holy Black)

*1579* Dutch provinces successfully revolt from Spain, creating United Netherlands

*1579* Ngola of Kingdom of Ndongo (in present-day Angola) attacked by Portuguese, with army composed mostly of Africans

*1580* In Mozambique, the Makua revolt against Portuguese

*c. 1580* Manchester, England, has flourishing market in wool trade; restrictions placed on use of cotton in cloth-making to protect sheep and wool industry

*1582* Gregorian calendar adopted in Papal States, Spain, Portugal, France, the Netherlands, and Scandinavia

*1582* University of Edinburgh founded

*1583* First insurance policies on life and property written in England

*1584* Sir Walter Raleigh discovers and annexes Virginia

*1585* English establish short-lived colony of Roanoke (in present-day North Carolina)

*1587* Second colony founded at Roanoke; colonists mysteriously disappear

*1585* Queen Elizabeth takes the Netherlands under her protection

*1587* Pope Sixtus V promises financial aid to send Spanish Armada against England

*1587* Japan banishes Portuguese missionaries

*1588* England defeats "invincible" Spanish Armada

*1589* Francis Drake, with 150 ships, fails to take Lisbon for England

*1590* Emperor of Morocco annexes Timbuktu

*1590* Moroccan army invades Songhai empire (eastern Mali)

*1590* Portuguese defeated by alliance of Matamba and Ndongo (Angola)

*1591* In Brazilian regions of Bahia and Pernambuco, Europeans first observe and denounce Africans for syncretizing Catholicism with African religions

*1592* Portuguese military routed by the Zimba in Zambezi Valley in East Africa

*1593* Shakespeare completes *Titus Andronicus,* first of two plays with major Moor character; *Othello* completed a decade later

*1593* Fort Jesus at Mombasa, Kenya, constructed by Portuguese

*1594* England breaks Portugal's trade monopoly with India

*1595* Dutch begin to colonize East Indies

*1595* Sir Walter Raleigh explores 300 miles up Orinoco River, Venezuela

*1596* Tomatoes from America introduced in England

1597 Dutch found Batavia, Java

1597 Parliament prescribes sentences of transportation to English colonies for convicted criminals

1597 Dutch conquer Mauritius

1597 Outbreak of plague in Spain

1598 Isabel de Olvera, free black woman, accompanies Spanish expedition to New Mexico

c. 1600 Keira dynasty founded in Darfur (Sudan/Chad)

1600 English East India Company founded

1602 Basque captain Sebastián Vizcaíno, sailing for Spain, explores coastline from Mexico as far north as Monterey Bay

1602 States-General of the Netherlands grants Dutch East India Company 21-year monopoly to expand trade and maintain close relations with its Asian colonies

1602 King James I succeeds Queen Elizabeth I of England

1602 England claims Barbados as colony

1603 Mathieu Da Costa, free black, guides French through parts of Canada and Lake Champlain region of New York State

1604 Treaty of London concludes 20-year Anglo-Spain War

1605 In preface to *Don Juan*, Miguel de Cervantes commemorates importance of Juan Latino to Spanish literature

1605–94 Largest and best-organized *quilombo* (Brazilian settlement), Palmares, established by escaped slaves in Pernambuco, Brazil; flourishes for nearly a century

1606 Virginia Company of London sends three ships of 120 colonists to Virginia, founding Jamestown in 1607

1607 Dutch launch failed attack at Portuguese outpost in Mozambique

1608 Samuel de Champlain establishes French settlement at Quebec

1609 Truce between Spain and the Netherlands

1609 Henry Hudson explores North American coast for the Netherlands

| AFRICAN-AMERICAN | GLOBAL / AFRICAN DIASPORAN |
|---|---|
|  | *1610* Jesuit Peter Claver arrives in New Granada (Colombia), protests bad treatment of slaves |
|  | *1611* Shakespeare completes *The Tempest*, set in Bermuda colony |
| *1612* Tobacco planted in Virginia | *1611* King James Version of the Bible published |
| *1612* Dutch use Manhattan as fur trading center |  |
| *1613* English prevent French settlement in Maryland and Nova Scotia |  |
| *1613* Jan Rodriguez, free black sailor working for Dutch fur trading company, left alone on Manhattan Island to live and trade with Native Americans |  |
| *1614* Spanish colonial law prohibits buying goods from slaves |  |
|  | *1616* Sir Walter Raleigh released from prison to lead expedition to Guiana (Guyana) in search of El Dorado |
|  | *1616* Catholic Church prohibits Galileo from further scientific work |
|  | *1617* Dutch purchase Gorée Island from natives |
|  | *1618* Jesuit Claver instructs and baptizes slaves in Colombia; Church estimates he performed more than 300,000 baptisms in his lifetime |
| *1619* Dutch ship brings first 20 enslaved Africans to Jamestown, Virginia |  |
| *1619* First colonial assembly held in Jamestown, Virginia | *1620* Pilgrims leave England, bound for North America, aboard *Mayflower* |
|  | *c. 1620* Manchester textile manufacturers begin to add small amounts of cotton in cloth-making process (origins of cotton industry) |
|  | *1620* Black Catholic clergyman Martin de Porres founds orphanage and foundling hospital in Lima, Peru |
|  | *1621* Dutch West India Company founded |

*1622* English and Dutch fleets blockade Portuguese port at Mozambique

*1623* Dutch found New Netherland in North America

*1623* English start settlement at St. Kitts in Leeward Islands

*1624* First known African child born free in English colonies, William Tucker, baptized in Virginia

*1624* English Parliament declares monopolies illegal

*1625* Enslaved Africans arrive in New Amsterdam (Manhattan) with Dutch West India Company and become city's first municipal labor force—clearing timber, cutting lumber, cultivating farmland, and constructing roads and fortifications

*1625* French and enslaved Africans settle the Antilles and Cayenne

*1625* Colony founded on Barbados using labor of enslaved Africans

*1626* Dutch "buy" Manhattan Island from Native Americans for 60 guilders (approximately 24 dollars)

*1626* French settle on Senegal River

*1627* English King Charles I grants charter to Guiana Company

*1628* English, accompanied by enslaved Africans, settle Nevis in Leeward Islands

*1629* English found Massachusetts Bay Colony

*1629* Responding to Portuguese invasion, Nzinga (Dona Ana de Sousa), Queen of Angola, launches counterattack

*1632* Ethiopia expels Jesuit missionaries, ending attempts to convert country to Roman Catholicism

*1632* Charles I grants charter for Maryland colony, under Lord Baltimore

*1632* English settle Antigua and Montserrat

*1632* First coffee shop opens in London

*1633* Dutch settle on Connecticut River

*1634* Slavery introduced in Maryland

*1634* Dutch capture Curaçao

*1635* Tobacco use in France restricted to doctors' prescriptions

*1636* Dutch minister Everardus Bogardus summons a teacher from Holland to Manhattan Island "to train the youth of the Dutch and the Blacks in the knowledge of Jesus Christ," today's Collegiate School for Boys

*1637* English Captain John Underhill leads massacre of Pequot settlement in Connecticut

*1637* French settle St. Louis, on Senegal River, West Africa

*1637* Dutch expel Portuguese from African Gold Coast

*1639* First enslaved Africans arrive in Connecticut and Delaware

*1641* Massachusetts first colony to legalize slavery

*1641* Mathias de Sousa, African indentured servant from England, elected to Maryland's General Assembly

*1641* Cotton manufacturing begins in Manchester, England, with cotton used primarily for padding of jerkins, pillows, and mattresses

*1642* Fugitive Slave Law enacted in Virginia; runaways to be branded with letter R after second escape attempt

*1642* English theaters closed by order of Puritans

*1642* First English Civil War

*1643* New England Confederation adopts Fugitive Slave Law

*1643* Five-year-old Louis XIV succeeds his father, Louis XIII, upon his death

*1644* Led by Captain Underhill, Dutch soldiers massacre Indian settlement in Bronx

*1644* Eleven enslaved Africans receive freedom and farmland grants in New Amsterdam from Dutch colonists as compensation for support in Dutch-Indian Wars

*1645* Merchant ships from Barbados arrive in Boston and exchange cargoes of enslaved Africans, sugar, and tobacco for rum and manufactured products

*1645* Sugar production increases slave population in Barbados from about 500 to more than 6,000

*1645* Swedes take control of slave trade from the Portuguese on Gold Coast (Ghana) and construct Fort Christianborg

*1646* First English Civil War ends, with Oliver Cromwell ultimately victorious at conclusion of Third English Civil War (1651)

| AFRICAN-AMERICAN | GLOBAL/AFRICAN DIASPORAN |
|---|---|
| | *1646* English Parliament demands religious reforms, effectively a repudiation of Catholicism |
| | *1646* English and enslaved Africans settle Bahamas |
| | *1646* First projection lantern (*laterna magica*) invented in Germany |
| | *1647* Yellow fever spreads in Barbados |
| | *1647* Dutch ship *Haarlem* runs aground at Table Bay (Cape Town, South Africa); crew builds fort on beach |
| *1649* New Amsterdam governor Peter Stuyvesant coordinates sale of enslaved Africans to planters in Barbados and other Caribbean Islands | *1649* Charles I beheaded; England declared Commonwealth |
| *1650* Connecticut legalizes slavery | *1650* Parliament enacts English Navigation Act against Dutch; Peter Stuyvesant defies prohibition and continues to provide slaves to Barbados |
| | *1650* Dutch colonize Cape of Good Hope (South Africa); settlers known as Boers (farmers) |
| *1651* Free African Anthony Johnson given Virginia land grant | |
| *1652* Massachusetts requires all African and Indian servants to serve in colonial militia | |
| *1652* Rhode Island enacts first anti-slavery law in colonies, limiting term of servitude to ten years | |
| *1653* Enslaved workers build wall across Manhattan Island (now Wall Street) to protect Dutch colony from British invasion | *1653* English defeat Dutch in naval warfare off Texel and Portland, Holland |
| | *1654* Portuguese, led by Afro-Brazilian General Henrique Dias, oust Dutch from Recife and Pernambuco |
| | *1654* Treaty of Westminster ends First Anglo-Dutch war |

**1655** Dutch slave ship, *Witte Paert* (*White Horse*), arrives with 300 Africans from Guinea, the first slaves shipped directly to New Amsterdam from Africa

**1655–1740** Series of slave rebellions against English lead to founding of runaway Maroon communities in mountains of Jamaica

**1655** English seize Cayman Islands and Jamaica from Spain, but fail to capture Maroons

**1655** Plague strikes Angola; several thousands die

**1656** Fearing slave uprisings, Massachusetts reverses 1652 statute permitting blacks to carry arms; Connecticut, New Hampshire, and New York soon follow

**1656** First London opera house opens

**1657** Virginia adds statutes to Fugitive Slave Law, including fining those who harbor runaway slaves 30 pounds of tobacco for every night of shelter

**1657** Danes take possession of Fort Christianborg (Gold Coast) from Swedes

**1657** Chocolate drinks introduced in London

**1658** New Amsterdam enslaved workers construct settlement and road to New Haarlem

**1658** Dutch abandon Mauritius

**1659** Saint-Louis, Senegal, oldest colonial city on western African coast, founded

**1660** Council of Foreign Plantations ordered by King Charles II of England to find ways to convert enslaved Africans to Christianity

**1661** Coronation of Charles II, King of England

**1662** Virginia enacts law to make slave status of children born to a white male and a black woman dependent upon the mother's status

**1663** Revolt planned by slaves and indentured servants uncovered in Gloucester County, Virginia

**1663** Charles II grants charters to Carolina and Rhode Island colonies

**1663** Louis XIV makes New France (Canada) royal province

**1664** Slave ship *Gideon* arrives in New Amsterdam with 290 men, women, and children; residents complain that there is not enough food to feed them

**1664** French found Compagnie des Indes occidentales to control French trade in the Americas, West Africa, and West Indies

*1664* Dutch surrender New Netherland to English, who divide and name colonies New York (after James II, Duke of York) and New Jersey and legalize slavery

*1664* Maryland bans marriages between white women and black men

*1665* Duke of York major shareholder in Royal African Company slave-trading enterprise; "Duke's Laws" grant port privileges and warehouse priority to ships engaged in slave trade

*1665* Portuguese win battle of Mbwila in Angola

*1666* Dutch and French declare war on England

*1666* French capture St. Christopher, Montserrat, and Antigua

*1667* Virginia law states Christian baptism does not alter slave status

*1667* British Act to Regulate the Negroes on the British Plantation in the colonies forbids leaving plantations on Sundays and bans signaling instruments like whistles, horns, and drums

*1667* Secret treaty between France and England against Spain

*1667* Buenos Aires reports scarcity of slaves due to disease

*1669* Barbados receiving 5,000 enslaved Africans per year

*1670* Virginia law declares all non-Christians who arrive by ship may be enslaved

*1670* Massachusetts permits sale of children of enslaved Africans into bondage

*1670* French royal decree encourages French shippers into slave trade; French West Indies imports 3,000 slaves annually

*1672* Virginia enacts legislation making legal the killing of a slave during apprehension

*1672* France declares war on the Netherlands

*1672* Royal African Company chartered with Duke of York as governor

*1673* French Senegal Company founded

*1673* Slave uprisings in Jamaica (again in 1678, 1682, 1685, and 1690)

*1674* French evacuate Madagascar

*1674* Charles II names former buccaneer Sir Henry Morgan deputy governor of Jamaica

*1675* War between Sweden and Denmark

*1676* Nathaniel Bacon leads unsuccessful rebellion of whites and blacks against English colonial government in Virginia

*1677* The Akwamu (southeastern Ghana) defeat coastal capital of Accra (Nkran)

*1678* Peace treaty between France and Spain

*1679* Slave uprising in Haiti

*1680* Virginia law forbids all blacks from carrying arms and requires enslaved blacks to carry certificates when leaving owner's plantation

*c. 1680* Slaves of Royal African Company (RAC) marked "DY" with burning iron on right breast, for Duke of York, chairman of RAC

*1680* The Ga migrate from Accra plain to Anecho, Dahomey

*c. 1680* Expansion in sugar and tobacco production increase demand for slaves in the Caribbean and American mainland

*1681* King Charles II grants William Penn royal charter; Pennsylvania established

*1682* Virginia declares that all imported servants are slaves

*1682* René-Robert Cavelier, Sieur de La Salle, claims territory from Quebec to mouth of Mississippi River for France, naming it Louisiana

*1682* New York enacts its first slave codes restricting freedom of movement and trade

*1683* Peace treaty between William Penn and Native Americans

*1683* Spain declares war on France

*1684* Bermuda established as British crown colony

*1685* New York law prohibits enslaved Africans and Native Americans from meeting in groups larger than four or carrying weapons

*1685* Inhabitants of Pate (Kenya) rebel against Portuguese

*1685* French settle in Texas

*1686* Dominion of New England formed to improve control of British colonies in North America

*1686* French annex Madagascar

*1687* Brandenburg (German) colony established at Arguin Island (West Africa)

*1688* Quakers in Germantown, Pennsylvania, publish first manifesto condemning slavery in colonial North America

*1688* Lloyds of London provides insurance for ships carrying commodities and slaves

*1689* William III and Mary II proclaimed King and Queen of England

*1689* Louis XIV declares war on Britain, approves importation of slaves to New France (Canada)

*1690* South Carolina assembly passes its first slave law

*1690* The Ashanti unite to establish Ashanti kingdom

*1691* Virginia law punishes white men and women for marrying blacks or Indians; children of such liaisons become property of church for 30 years

*1691* Plymouth Colony joins Massachusetts Bay Colony

*1692* Abuna (Bishop) Synnada replaces Abuna Marcus as head of Ethiopian Church

*1692* Earthquake hits Jamaica, killing more than 1,500

*1693* Runaway Africans who escaped slavery in British colonies and fled to Florida declared free by Royal Spanish decree

*1693* Slaves mine gold discovered at Minas Gerais, Brazil

*1693* Carolina divided into North and South colonies

*1694* Successful rice crop in South Carolina colony spurs importation of enslaved laborers

*1694* Bank of England founded

*1694* Gold found in Taubaté, Brazil, increasing demand for slaves

*1695* Rev. Samuel Thomas establishes first school for Africans in colonies

*1695* In Palmares, Brazil, African commander Zumbi captured and killed

*1695* Changamire defeats Portuguese in Zimbabwe

*1696* American Quakers warn members that they may be expelled for owning slaves

*1696* Board of Trade and Plantations founded in England

*1697* André Brue of France attempts to colonize West Africa

*1698* Chocolate House opens in London, becomes headquarters of Tory Party

*1698* Royal African Company loses its monopoly; Bristol and Liverpool officially become slaving ports

*1699* Pierre Lemoyne founds first French settlements in Louisiana

*1700* Publication of Samuel Sewall's *The Selling of Joseph*, first American protest against slavery

*1700* Enslaved African population in the American colonies reaches 28,000, 23,000 of whom are in the South

*1700* Great Northern War commences as Russia, allied with Denmark-Norway, and Saxony-Poland challenge Sweden's supremacy in Baltic region

*1700* Franciscans of Guinea (Guinea-Bissau) condemn slave trade

*1701* Catechism made mandatory for all slaves in Guiana

*1701* The Asante battle the Denkyira in competition for Dutch trade at Elmina

*1702* New York law allows enslaved Africans to be whipped 40 lashes and prohibits enslaved Africans from testifying against free whites or gathering in public in groups larger than three

*1702* *Asiento* (license to trade in slavery) granted to French Guinea Company for slave trade to supply at least 4,800 slaves per year to Spanish colonies in the Americas for ten years

*1702* Dutch Trekboers clash against Xhosa for herds crossing Boer farms

*1705* Virginia law declares all enslaved Africans real estate and not chattels

*1706* French and Spanish troops try unsuccessfully to capture Charleston, South Carolina

*1706* Ethiopian emperor Iyasu I assassinated; son Takla Haimanot I succeeds him

*1707* Union of England and Scotland creates Kingdom of Great Britain

*1708* Africans in South Carolina outnumber Europeans, making it first English colony in North America with more blacks than whites

*1708* Agaja ascends to King of the Fon (Dahomey)

*1710* Mauritius abandoned by Dutch

*1710* Slave conspiracy in Brazil instigated by Muslim slaves

*1711* Slave market opens in New York City at corner of Wall Street and East River

*1711* England's Queen Anne overrules Quaker-inspired Pennsylvania colonial law prohibiting slavery

*1711* War between Tuscarora Indians and settlers in North Carolina; more than 100 enslaved Africans escape

*1711* Portuguese and African soldiers battle French at Rio de Janeiro, Brazil; Portuguese and Africans fight indigenous villages along Amazon

| AFRICAN-AMERICAN | GLOBAL / AFRICAN DIASPORAN |
|---|---|
| *1712* Slave uprising in New York City leaves nine whites killed; 6 Africans committed suicide, 20 were hanged, and 3 were burned. | *1712* Population of Jamaica 3,500 Europeans and 42,000 Africans |
| *1712* New York City law prohibits free blacks from inheriting land | *1713* Peace of Utrecht signed by Spain and Great Britain opens British trade to Spanish America |
| | *1714* French Senegal Company establishes slave posts in new ports on Guinea coast (Guinea-Bissau / Senegal) |
| *1715* Indians and fugitive slaves attack white settlements in South Carolina | *1715* French take over former Dutch post at Mauritius |
| *1715* Rhode Island legalizes slavery | *1715* Ricardo O'Farrill opens slave market in Havana, Cuba |
| *1716* First enslaved Africans arrive in French Louisiana | *1716* Boers wage war against South African Bushmen in territorial expansion |
| *1718* French found New Orleans, which by 1721 has more enslaved black males than white men | *1718* Quadruple Alliance signed by France, England, Holland, and Holy Roman Empire |
| | *1720* Coffee planted in Martinique, an island known primarily for sugar production |
| | *c. 1720* West Indian rum replacing French brandy as popular alcoholic beverage |
| *1721* Dr. Zabdiel Boylston of Boston uses African smallpox inoculation on his son, disputes protests that the technique, used by enslaved Africans, is barbaric and sinful. Boston smallpox epidemic, which caused 884 deaths, dramatically decreases following inoculations | *1723* Sultan of Kilwa seeks Portuguese aid in expelling Omani Arabs from East African coast |
| *1724* Code Noir enacted in France's Louisiana territory to regulate slavery | |
| *1724* Boston imposes nightly curfew on blacks and Indians | *1726* First of several slave rebellions occurs in Suriname |

*1727* Enslaved Africans and Indians revolt in Middlesex and Gloucester counties in Virginia

*1737* White coopers (barrel makers) petition New York colonial legislature to prohibit "breeding slaves" for trades

*1738* First permanent black settlement in North America established by fugitive Africans at Gracia Real de Santa Teresa de Mosé, Florida

*1739* Slave revolt occurs in Stono, South Carolina; 21 whites and an estimated 44 blacks killed

*1727* Coffee first planted in Brazil

*1727* Agadja, King of Dahomey, conquers city of Ouidah on Slave Coast (Benin); controls exports of 15,000 to 20,000 enslaved Africans annually

*1728* Diamonds found at Minas Gerais, Brazil

*1729* Portugal loses Mombasa in East Africa to Arabs

*1729* English court rules that Christian "baptism doth not bestow freedom" on colonial slaves; nor are slaves brought to England to be free

*c. 1730* Cotton manufacturing in Manchester, England, challenges, then eclipses, its production of wool, linen, and silk

*1730* John and Charles Wesley found Methodist sect at Oxford, England

*1730* Empress Mentaub (Menetewab), of Portuguese and Ethiopian descent, rules Ethiopia

*1733* British Molasses Act prohibits American trade with French and Dutch West Indies

*1734* Koran translated into English by George Sale

*1738* Ghana-born Anton Wilhelm von Amo, black professor at University of Wittenberg, publishes Latin treatise on metaphysics

| AFRICAN-AMERICAN | GLOBAL/AFRICAN DIASPORAN |
|---|---|
| **1740** South Carolina enacts its most extensive slave code to ensure "the slave may be kept in due subjection and obedience," prohibiting assembly in groups, earning money, learning to read or write, and permitting owners to kill rebellious slaves | **1740** Lunda kingdom emerges in Kazembe (Zambia) |
| **1741** Enslaved Africans accused of plot to takeover New York City; 31 blacks and 4 whites convicted and executed | **1741** Tomas Navarro receives *asiento* ("assent," or license to trade in slavery) from Spain to supply enslaved Africans to Buenos Aires (Argentina) and Montevideo (Uruguay) |
| | **1742** West African born Jacobus Capitein, educated in Holland, publishes essay declaring slavery not contrary to Christian doctrine |
| | **1743** Pope Benedict XIV beatifies Benedict the Moor, patron saint of Palermo |
| **1746** Lucy Terry, an enslaved woman, composes "Bars Fight," first-known poem by an African American; poem first published in 1855 | **1747** The Yoruba triumph over the Dahomey |
| | **1750** Replacement of London-based Royal African Trading Company with Company of Merchants Trading to Africa gives more power to merchants from Bristol and Liverpool |
| | **1750** Kwasi Obodun (Kusi Obodum) becomes leader of the Asante (Ghana) |
| **1752** Benjamin Banneker, 21-year-old inventor, constructs one of first clocks in colonial America | **1752** First missionaries from the Society for Propagation of the Gospel in Foreign Parts arrive at the Cape Coast Castle (Ghana) |
| | **1754** Population of Haiti 172,000 Africans, 14,000 Europeans, 4,000 mixed race |
| | **1754** Ghanaian Philip Quaque (Kweku) sent to England for education; will become first African ordained priest in Church of England |

*1757* Olaudah Equiano, enslaved African born in Nigeria, arrives in Virginia from Barbados; he speaks of Middle Passage later in his autobiography, *Interesting Narrative of the Life of Olaudah Equiano, or Gustavus Vassa, the African*:

*1755* Brazilian colonial government declares enslavement of Amerindians illegal; creates more demand for enslaved Africans

"[Q]uite overpowered with horror and anguish, I fell motionless on the deck and fainted."

*1758* First congregation of enslaved Africans—the "Bluestone" or African Baptist Church—is founded on William Byrd III plantation, Mecklenburg, Virginia

*1758* School for free black children opens in Philadelphia

*1760* *A Narrative of the Uncommon Sufferings and Surprising Deliverance of Briton Hammon* first published autobiography by an enslaved African living in America

*1761* Jupiter Hammon's "An Evening Thought: Salvation by Christ with Penitential Cries," first published poem by an enslaved black poet in North America

*1762* Slave revolts in Guiana

*1763* Seven Year's War concludes with Treaty of Paris, France loses Senegal (except for island of Gorée) and most of its North American territory to Britain

*1763* Revolt in Dutch Guianese colony of Berbice, led by Cuffy, involves more than 2,500 enslaved Africans from two plantations

*1764* English Parliament passes Sugar Act, imposing taxes on sugar, coffee, and other goods imported by Americans, who protest taxation without representation

*1765* Parliament issues Stamp Act, taxing printed materials, such as newspapers, magazines, wills, marriage licenses, and playing cards

*1766* Protests by colonists lead Parliament to repeal Stamp Act, but new Declaratory Act confirms England's binding authority to rule over American colony

*1767* Birth of Father José Mauricio, Afro-Brazilian composer and organist

*1769* Portuguese try unsuccessfully to recapture Mombasa

*1770* Crispus Attucks, an escaped enslaved African, first person killed by British in Boston Massacre

*c. 1770* Coffee introduced as plantation crop in Cuba

*c. 1770* Alafin Abiodun, Yoruba leader of the Oyo (Nigeria), controls estimated 600 towns and villages, and gains great profits from slave trade

*c. 1770* Cotton manufacturing, using new equipment (and by the 1780s, steam power), ushers in Industrial Revolution in England

*1771* French Minister of Colonies issues edict against granting French citizenship to persons of mixed-race African ancestry

*1772* After escape in England, enslaved African James Somersett, owned by Boston Customs official, freed by British judge

*1772* In milestone case of American slave James Somerset, English court rules that a slave cannot be seized against his will on England's soil; many slaveowners fear the ruling could spread to the American colonies

*1773* Phillis Wheatley's book *Poems on Various Subjects, Religious and Moral* published in England; the following year, she writes to Native American minister Samson Occom:

*1773* In law considered enlightened, "people of color" from Brazil forbidden to enter Portugal

"In every human Breast, God has implanted a Principle, which we call Love of Freedom; it is impatient of Oppression, and pants for Deliverance; . . . "

*1773* Silver Bluff Baptist Church founded in South Carolina

*1773* Enslaved Africans in Boston petition governor, council, and House of Representatives for freedom

*1774* Methodist founder John Wesley publishes *Thoughts Upon Slavery*, concluding England's worst crime is its continuing indulgence in slave trade

*1775* General George Washington reverses his ban and permits enslaved and free Africans to enlist in the Continental Army; between 5,000 and 7,000 join; British Governor of Virginia promises freedom to those who fight for British

*1775* Algeria declares freedom to slaves, unless they are owned by the government

*1775* Pennsylvania Abolition Society, the first in North America, meets in Philadelphia

*1776* Thomas Jefferson appeases slaveholders by removing references to slavery and slave trade from Declaration of Independence

*1776* France contracts with Sultan of Kilwa (island off Tanzania) to receive 1,000 slaves annually for next 100 years

*1776* First attempt to end slave trade introduced in English Parliament, but fails

*1777* Vermont abolishes slavery

*1777* French Minister of Colonies refuses to allow blacks to enter France, because "they marry Europeans . . . and colors are mixed"

*1779* Jean Baptiste Point du Sable, black Canadian born in West Indies, establishes trading post that later becomes city of Chicago

*1779* Last public sale of black slave in England takes place in Liverpool

*1779* 500 Haitian soldiers join American colonists and French soldiers in an unsuccessful effort to drive British from Savannah

*1780* Merchant Paul Cuffee and six others petition the Massachusetts legislature to end taxation without representation

*1780* Pennsylvania abolitionists push legislature to pass An Act for the Gradual Abolition of Slavery, first state statute to end slavery

*1780* James Derham, first black recognized to have regularly practiced medicine in North America

*1781* Intelligence reports of enslaved African James Armistead help defeat British at the Battle of Yorktown

*1781* Kingdom of Oyo goes to war against the Dahomey

*1781* Twenty-six blacks among 44 settlers founding city of Los Angeles, California

*1781* 133 enslaved Africans are thrown overboard from British slave ship *Zong*

*1783* General Washington insists on reparations for loss of slave owner's "property" after British General Sir Guy Carleton insists on keeping his promise of freedom to 3,000 enslaved Africans who fought for British

*1783* Owners of *Zong* sue insurers for value of 133 slaves, but lose in court

*1783* The British transport 3,000 Black Loyalists who fought with them during American Revolution to Nova Scotia

*1784* Christian missionary George Liele, first black Baptist in Georgia, travels from Savannah to Jamaica to found new Baptist congregation

## FROM INDEPENDENCE TO CIVIL WAR

*1784* New York African Society, a spiritual and benevolent association, formed in Manhattan

*1784* Prince Hall's African Lodge #459 granted Masonic charter by Grand Lodge of England

*1784* Connecticut and Rhode Island pass gradual emancipation acts, other northern states follow

*1785* New York Society for Promoting the Manumission of Slaves founded; includes civic leaders such as John Jay and Alexander Hamilton

*1785* James Watt installs steam engine in English cotton-spinning factory

*1787* Continental Congress outlaws slavery in Northwest Territory (incoming states located north of Ohio River and east of Mississippi River)

*1787* Violinist Chevalier Joseph de Saint-Georges, freeborn in Guadeloupe, composes *La fille-garçon* in Paris

*1787* Constitutional Convention drafts US Constitution, including fugitive slave clause and provision that counts blacks as three-fifths of a person for taxation and representation purposes

*1787* Constitutional compromise of 1787 puts an end to the slave import trade by 1808

*1787* New Jersey and Rhode Island abolish slave trade; Massachusetts, Connecticut, and New York soon follow

*1787* African Free School founded by New York Manumission Society

*1787* Jupiter Hammon's sermon, "An Address to the Negroes in the State of New York," published

*1787* Richard Allen and Absalom Jones with other ex-slaves and Quakers form Free African Society, quasi-religious benevolent organization offering fellowship and mutual aid to "free Africans and their descendants"

*1788* New York State legislature passes law prohibiting sale of slaves brought into state after 1785, and grants slaves right to trial by jury for capital offenses

*1788* Société des Amis des Noirs (Society of the Friends of Blacks) established in France for abolition of slave trade

*1788* First known abolitionist paintings, contrasting benevolence of Africans and barbarous behavior of Europeans, exhibited at Royal Academy in London

*1788* William Pitt and William Wilberforce appear before Parliament to demand abolition of slave trade

*1788* Gustavus Vassa (Olaudah Equiano) presents petition to end slave trade to Queen Charlotte and British Parliament

| AFRICAN-AMERICAN | GLOBAL/AFRICAN DIASPORAN |
|---|---|
| *1789* First session of Congress established by ratification of Constitution, held in New York City, first capital of the United States; George Washington inaugurated president | *1789* French Revolution begins, as Paris mob storms Bastille |
| *1789* Samuel Fraunces, West Indian proprietor of Fraunces Tavern, becomes steward at presidential mansion in New York | |
| *1789* John Jay, proponent of gradual manumission, becomes first chief justice of US Supreme Court | |
| *1789* US Congress approves first ten amendments to Constitution: Bill of Rights | |
| *1790* US Congress moves capital from New York, approving expenditures for slave labor to build new capitol buildings on an undeveloped region of the Potomac River in Virginia; Philadelphia becomes interim capital | *c. 1790* To preserve British monopoly on cotton manufacturing techniques, England prohibits exportation of machinery and manufacturing techniques |
| *1790* First US census places black population at 757,208, of whom 59,527 are free | *1790* Over 1,000 Black Loyalists, dissatisfied with conditions in Nova Scotia, resettle in Sierra Leone |
| *1791* Bill of Rights ratified | *1791* Haitian revolution begins, as slaves in Saint-Domingue rebel against French rule |
| | *1791* Slave uprising in Dominica upsets many in Britain, who use revolt to argue against abolition |
| | *1791* Britain grants charter to abolitionist Sierra Leone Company for purpose of establishing trade with new colony and overseeing its resettlement with free blacks |
| *1792* Benjamin Banneker's *Almanac* published in Philadelphia; first scientific book by an African American | *1793* In Haiti, France promises freedom to all those enslaved who will join French army against rebels |
| *1793* Congress passes first federal Fugitive Slave Law, authorizing any federal district or circuit judge or any state magistrate to determine status of an alleged fugitive | *1793* The Canadian legislature approves gradual abolition of enslaved Africans within Canada |

*1793* African-American baker Catherine Ferguson forms New York City's first Sunday school

*1794* Eli Whitney granted patent on cotton gin; its use increases demand for slave labor in southern states

*1794* Mother Bethel African Methodist Episcopal Church established in Philadelphia by Rev. Richard Allen

*1796* African-American members leave white John Street Methodist Church in New York and form Mother Zion Church, the Mother Church of the African Methodist Episcopal Zion denomination

*1799* New York State passes Gradual Abolition Act

*1800* US federal offices move from Philadelphia to Washington, DC

*1800* Inspired by Haitian Revolution, Gabriel Prosser and more than 1,000 enslaved supporters prepare to attack whites in Richmond, Virginia; Gov. James Monroe sends troops to stop revolt

*1794* Britain takes Martinique, Guadaloupe, and St. Lucia from French control

*1794* Work completed on Brazil's Church of São Francisco de Assis, distinguished by artwork of Afro-Portuguese sculptor Aleijadinho (born António Francisco Lisboa)

*1796* In Jamaica, Maroons try to incite general slave revolt; British troops capture 600 Maroons and ship them to Nova Scotia, and eventually to Sierra Leone

*1796* Slaves revolt in Saint Lucia; British end uprising by promising freedom to those who lay down their weapons

*1797* In South Africa, British troops wage war against the Xhosa, driving the natives across Fish River

*1797* British take Trinidad from Spain

*1798* England signs treaty with Toussaint L'Ouverture, recognizing Haiti as independent

*c. 1800* Ninety percent of cotton used in English manufacturing comes from Louisiana, Brazil, Guiana, and Surinam; less than 8 percent from "free areas," such as Turkey

*1800* Portuguese export 15,000 enslaved Africans per year from Mozambique

*1801* Freed African slave General Toussaint L'Ouverture conquers first French colony of Saint-Domingue (Haiti) and then Spanish colony of Santo Domingo (Dominican Republic); controls entire island of Hispaniola

| AFRICAN-AMERICAN | GLOBAL / AFRICAN DIASPORAN |
|---|---|
| | *1802* Napoleon sends French troops to reconquer Haiti; jails L'Ouverture and restores slavery |
| *1803* Haitian Revolution induces Napoleon to sell Louisiana Territory to US | *1803* Jean-Jacques Dessalines, successor to L'Ouverture, defeats Napoleon's forces; L'Ouverture dies in French prison |
| *1804* Black Laws enacted in Ohio | *1804* On January 1, Haiti declares its independence |
| | *1806* Rivalry leads to war between the Asante and Fante on Gold Coast (Ghana) |
| | *1807* Enslaved Muslims revolt in Bahia, Brazil (again in 1835) |
| | *1807* British Parliament abolishes transatlantic slave trade |
| | *1807* Pope Pius VII canonizes Benedict the Moor as first black Catholic saint |
| *1808* US outlaws transatlantic slave trade | *1808* British West Africa Squadron (Royal Navy) established to suppress slave trading |
| | *1809* French lose Cayenne and Martinique to British |
| | *1810* Cotton manufacturing exports in England surpass wool |
| | *1810* British seize Guadeloupe, last French colony in West |
| | *1811* War between British and Kaffirs in South Africa (again in 1818, 1834, 1835, and 1877) |
| | *1813* Sweden abolishes its slave trade |
| | *1814* Dutch cede Cape Colony (South Africa) to Great Britain |
| | *1814* Abdallah bin Ahmad al-Mazrui proclaims independence of Mombasa (Kenya) |

| | |
|---|---|
| | **1815** At Congress of Vienna, Portugal and Spain oppose British pressure to abolish slavery; Spain and Portugal approve acts to gradually abolish slavery |
| **1816** Richard Allen and associates found African Methodist Episcopal (AME) Church denomination | **1816** Argentina prohibits sale of slaves outside its borders |
| **1816** American Colonization Society founded by wealthy whites to repatriate free African Americans to Africa | |
| **1819** Spain cedes Florida to US to cancel $5 million debt | **1818** France declares slave trade illegal |
| **1820** Black leaders vote themselves out of white Methodist Episcopal Church and publish first AME Zion Church discipline | **1820** Afro-Russian poet Alexander Pushkin banished to the Caucasus after circulation of his 1817 poem "Vol'nost'" ("Ode to Liberty") |
| **1820** American Colonization Society's first ship, *Mayflower of Liberia*, arrives in Liberia; experiencing tropical illnesses, emigrants move on to Sierra Leone | **1820** Five million Europeans emigrate to US between 1820 and 1860 |
| **1821** African Grove Theater, first black acting troupe, established in New York City | |
| **1822** Denmark Vesey's plan to seize Charleston, South Carolina, to free enslaved Africans betrayed; he and 35 others executed | |
| **1823** Alexander Lucius Twilight, first African-American college graduate, earns degree from Middlebury College in Vermont | **1823** First Anglo-Asante War; ends with the Asante giving up claim to coast (Ghana) |
| **1823** African Grove Theater performs *The Drama of King Shotaway*, first play written by an African American, William Brown | **1823** The Anti-Slavery Society founded in London |
| | **1823** Abolition of slavery in Chile |
| **1824** Ira Aldridge, alumnus of African Grove Theater, begins illustrious acting career in Europe | **1824** African Americans in Liberia name their first settlement Monrovia, after US President James Monroe |

*1824* Slavery abolished in United Provinces of Central America (Honduras, Nicaragua, El Salvador, Costa Rica, Guatemala)

*1825* African-American actor Ira Aldridge, denied opportunities to perform in the US, stars in London as Oroonoko in *The Revolt of Surinam, or A Slave's Revenge*

*1825* France recognizes Haiti's independence, followed by Great Britain (1833) and US (1862)

*1826* Boers in Cape Colony (South Africa) threaten rebellion against British intentions to emancipate slaves, agree on gradual abolition plan by 1838

*1827* *Freedom's Journal*, first African American–owned newspaper, begins publishing in New York City with editors John Russwurm and Samuel Cornish:

"We wish to plead our own cause. Too long have others spoken for us."

*1827* Slavery abolished in state of New York

*1829* David Walker publishes his *Appeal*, calling for enslaved Africans to rise up and overthrow their oppressors:

*1829* Canada proclaims any slave who enters its border "immediately free" (see 1793)

"[G]o to work and enlighten your brethren!"

*1830* First National Negro Convention held in Philadelphia

*1829* Slavery abolished in Mexico

*1831* Nat Turner's rebellion in Virginia leads to repressive measures throughout the South

*1831* Alabama makes it illegal for enslaved or free blacks to preach

*1831* First African-American Female Literary Association organized in Philadelphia

*1832* Slave rebellion in British Guianese colony of Demerara helps revitalize international antislavery movement

*1833* African-American abolitionist Maria Stewart delivers address at African Masonic Hall in Boston:

"African rights and liberty is a subject that ought to fire the breast of every free man of color in these United States."

*1833* Ira Aldridge performs *Othello* in London with Ellen Terry, one of England's foremost actresses, playing Desdemona

*1833* British pass Slavery Abolition Act for the West Indies, but those formerly enslaved are indentured to their former owners in apprenticeship system until 1838

*1834* David Ruggles opens first US African-American bookstore in New York City

*1835* Boers begin "Trek" away from British-held Cape Colony into Transvaal and Natal

*1835* The Xhosa cede half of Natal (South Africa) to Great Britain

*1835* Slave revolts in three regions of Cuba: Jaruco, Matanzas, and Havana

*1835* Afro-Jamaican Edward Jordan elected to Jamaica House of Assembly in Kingston, three years before formal end of slavery

*1837* The Philadelphia Vigilance Committee organized to assist fugitive slaves

*1837* Afro-Cuban poet Juan Francisco Manzano publishes *La Música*

*1838* Boers equipped with canons and muskets kill 3,000 Zulu warriors in massacre known as the Battle of Blood River in Natal, suffering no fatalities

*1839* Pope Gregory XVI issues "In Supremo Apostolatus," papal bull condemning slavery and slave trade

*1840* US African-American population reaches 2,873,648

*1843* Henry Highland Garnet advocates armed rebellion against slavery at National Negro Convention in Buffalo, New York:

*1843* Samuel Jackman Prescod, son of a black mother and white father, is first nonwhite elected to House of Assembly in Barbados

"Brethren, arise, arise! Strike for your lives and liberties."

*1844* New Orleans-born African-American playwright Victor Séjour's first play, *Diégarias*, performed at Théâtre Français in Paris

*1844* Santo Domingo (Dominican Republic) declares itself separate republic from Haiti

*1844* Fante rulers agree to give Britain legal jurisdiction to their territory (Ghana)

*1845* Macon B. Allen becomes first African American admitted to the bar and begins law practice in Massachusetts

*1845* Afro-Frenchman Alexandre Dumas père publishes his second best-seller, *The Count of Monte Cristo*, following *The Three Musketeers*

*1847* Frederick Douglass elected president of New England Anti-Slavery Society and begins publishing newspaper *The North Star* in Rochester, New York

*1847* Republic of Liberia proclaimed; Joseph Jenkins Roberts, born in Virginia, elected its first president

*1847* David Jones Peck first African-American graduate of US medical school

*1848* French provisional government abolishes slavery in France's colonies

*1848* First Senegalese deputy to French National Assembly attends meeting in Paris

*1849* Harriet Tubman escapes slavery in Maryland and begins career as conductor on Underground Railroad

*1849* Libreville, French imitation of Freetown, founded for former slaves in Gabon

*1850* US African-American population reaches 3,636,808

*1850* Fugitive Slave Act makes any federal marshal or other official who does not arrest an alleged runaway slave liable to a fine of $1,000; anti-slavery citizens protest obligation to enforce slavery

*1850* Lucy Ann Stanton, first African-American woman to earn bachelor's degree, graduates from Oberlin College in Ohio

*1851* Sojourner Truth delivers "Ain't I a Woman?" Speech at Women's Rights Convention in Akron, Ohio:

*1851* Slavery abolished in Colombia and Panama

> "If the first woman God ever made was strong enough to turn the world upside down all alone, these women together ought to be able to turn it back."

*1851* British forces attack and occupy Lagos, Nigeria

*1852* Harriet Beecher Stowe publishes *Uncle Tom's Cabin*, strengthening anti-slavery movement

*1852* Slavery ends in Ecuador

*1852* Martin R. Delany publishes *The Condition, Elevation, Emigration and Destiny of the Colored People in the United States*, recommending emigration out of US

*1852* Afrikaners in the Transvaal permitted "to manage their own affairs" without interference of British government

*1853* Slavery ends by law in Uruguay

*1853* *The Lady of the Camellias*, first play by Alexandre Dumas fils, performed in Paris

*1853* Abolition of slavery in Argentina

*1854* Ashmun Institute (later Lincoln University) founded in Oxford, Pennsylvania, becomes first black college for young black men

*1854* Edward Jordan first Afro-Jamaican elected mayor of Kingston

*1854* Slavery abolished in Venezuela

*1855* In Gambia, war erupts between the Marabout and the Soninke, who were major suppliers of Atlantic slave trade

*1855* Slavery abolished in Peru

*1856* Natal (South Africa) chartered as British Crown colony; indentured laborers from India introduced in 1860

*1857* US Supreme Court rules in *Dred Scott v. Sandford* that blacks have no rights that whites are obliged to respect

*1859* White abolitionist John Brown leads raid on Harpers Ferry federal arsenal with 21 others, including five African Americans, to arm enslaved blacks; most killed, captured, or fled within 36 hours; Brown is hanged

*1859* *The Origin of Species* by Charles Darwin introduces evolutionary theory of human development; used to support myth of white supremacy

| AFRICAN-AMERICAN | GLOBAL/AFRICAN DIASPORAN |
|---|---|
| **1859** Harriet E. Wilson publishes first African-American novel, *Our Nig; or Sketches from the Life of a Free Black* | **1859** In Brazil, poet and former slave Luis Gama publishes *Primeiras Trovas Burlescas (First Comic Ballads)*, collection of scathing satires on denial of African ancestry among Brazilians |
| **1860** Abraham Lincoln elected president of US | **1860** 14 million Europeans immigrate to US between 1860 and 1900 |
|  | **1860** Indentured workers from India arrive in South Africa |
| **1861** Civil War begins when Confederates fire on Union forces at Fort Sumter, South Carolina | **1861** Great Britain declares neutrality regarding American Civil War |
|  | **1861** British forces invade Porto-Novo (Benin) |
|  | **1861** Slavery abolished in Bolivia |
| **1862** Congress mandates public education in District of Columbia for black and white children aged 6 to 14 | **1862** Cotton industry in Central and South America imports indentured workers from Asia; plantations established on Pacific Asian islands to meet demand because of lost production caused by American Civil War |
|  | **1862** British ignore Ethiopian emperor Theodore II's request for an alliance against Muslims; in turn, Theodore II jails British consul |
| **1863** Wilberforce University in Ohio (founded in 1856) becomes first college run by African Americans when Daniel A. Payne becomes president | **1863** Second Anglo-Asante War; leads to British control of the gold trade and annexation of present-day southern Ghana as part of Gold Coast colony in 1902 |
| **1863** Emancipation Proclamation takes effect on January 1; authorizes recruitment and use of African-American troops in Civil War | **1863** Slavery abolished in Dutch Surinam |
| **1863** Black 54th Regiment of Massachusetts storms Fort Wagner in South Carolina |  |

*1863* Frederick Douglass delivers "Men of Color, To Arms!" speech in Rochester, New York:

"Who would be free themselves must strike the blow."

*1864* Congress authorizes equal pay, equipment, and healthcare for African-American Union troops

*1864* Disruption in cotton production in US during Civil War leads to increased production in Egypt

*1864* *The New Orleans Tribune*, first daily African-American newspaper, publishes in English and French

*1865* Abraham Lincoln signs Thirteenth Amendment, outlawing slavery throughout US

*1865* Sahle Mariam, son of deposed king of Showa (in Ethiopia), reclaims Showa and declares himself king, though he recognizes Emperor Theodore II as his overlord

*1865* Congress establishes the Freedmen's Bureau to assist emancipated blacks in their transition to freedom and Freedman's Bank to promote savings and thrift

*1865* Ex-Confederates from US arrive in Brazil to start their own colony, Vila dos Americanos, primarily to produce cotton with slave labor

*1865* Confederate general Robert E. Lee surrenders to Ulysses S. Grant, effectively ending the Civil War

*1865* On June 19, Union Major General Gordon Granger reads US General Order #3 in Galveston, notifying Texans that slaves have been set free; annual Juneteenth celebrations begin in Texas the following year and spread to other states

*1865* Abraham Lincoln assassinated

*1865* Ku Klux Klan, formed in Pulaski, Tennessee, by six educated Confederate veterans, begins campaign of terror against blacks

## CREATING THE NEW NEGRO

*1866* Fisk University founded in Nashville, Tennessee

| AFRICAN-AMERICAN | GLOBAL/AFRICAN DIASPORAN |
|---|---|
| *1866* Reconstruction Congress overrides President Andrew Johnson's veto and enacts Civil Rights Act of 1866 | *1866* In Madrid, Junta de Información (Board of Information) meets, bringing together Spanish officials and delegates from Cuba and Puerto Rico to begin discussions on political reform and gradual abolition of slavery in two colonies |
| *1866* Congress approves Fourteenth Amendment to Constitution, granting citizenship to African Americans | |
| *1866* Congress authorizes the creation of four all-black regiments in US Army that become known as Buffalo Soldiers | |
| *1866* African-American jockey Abe Hawkins rides winners at Belmont and Saratoga | |
| *1867* Morehouse College and Howard University founded | |
| *1868* Black candidates elected to state legislatures and fill other governmental posts | *1868* The Asante and Fante ally to form Fante Confederation in Dutch-controlled west African coastal region (Ghana) |
| | *1868* King of Dahomey cedes Cotonou (Benin) to France to prevent Britain from gaining control |
| *1869* Joseph Rainey of South Carolina becomes first black elected to US House of Representatives | *1869* Vine rubber first exported from Angola |
| *1869* Fifteenth Amendment forbids denial of vote on basis of race, color, or previous condition of servitude | |
| *1870* Hiram Revels of Mississippi becomes first black US senator | *1870* Abolition of slavery in Paraguay |
| *1870* US African-American population 12.7 percent of total US population: 4,880,009 | |
| *1872* Pinckney Benton Stewart Pinchback becomes first African American to serve as state governor, serving in Louisiana | |

*1873* P. B. S. Pinchback defends election to US Senate, but is not seated:

*1873* Slavery abolished in Puerto Rico

> "[I]f I cannot enter the Senate except with bated breath and on bended knees, I prefer not to enter at all."

*1875* Forty-fourth US Congress convenes with eight African-American members

*1875* Civil Rights Act of 1875 enacted by Congress, forbidding discrimination in hotels, trains, and other public spaces, and barring disqualification of jurors on basis of race

*1874* British burn Asante capital of Kumasi and declare Gold Coast (Ghana) a Crown colony

*1876* Edward Alexander Bouchet first African American to earn doctorate in physics

*1876* African-American Lewis Latimer makes the technical drawings for Alexander Graham Bell's telephone patent application

*1876* Ethiopian forces defeat Egyptians near Gura, ending Egypt's attempt to annex region

*1877* Compromise of 1877 effectively ends Reconstruction, with federal troops withdrawn from the South, halting federal efforts to protect civil rights of African Americans

*1877* Afro-Brazilian author José do Patrocínio publishes *Motta Coqueiro*, novel about racial tensions that lead to murder on Brazilian plantation

*1878* Exodusters, former black slaves, begin migrating to Kansas from southern states to escape racist violence and oppression

*1879* Cocoa first planted in Gold Coast

*1880* De Beers mining corporation formed by Cecil Rhodes (Zimbabwe)

*1881* Tennessee passes law requiring separate railway cars for blacks and whites

*1881* Slave raids from Dahomey into Yorubaland (Nigeria) reported regularly

*1881* Transvaal Boers repel British attack

*1881* Booker T. Washington opens Normal School for Colored Teachers in Tuskegee, Alabama (later Tuskegee Institute)

*1882* Lewis Latimer patents carbon filament for electric lamp and begins working with Thomas Edison next year

*1882* British-French agreement reached regarding borders of Sierra Leone and Guinea

*1883* US Supreme Court declares Civil Rights Act of 1875 invalid

*1883* German chancellor Bismarck approves German plan to purchase land for trading stations along coast of South-West Africa

| African-American | Global / African Diasporan |
|---|---|
| **1883** Fiftieth Congress has no black members as racial intimidation keeps black voters from polls | **1883** German settlements appear in Angra Pequeña (Namibia); Britain warns Germany that it is infringing on British territory |
| **1884** Granville Woods founds Woods Electric Company and produces 35 patented devices over next 20 years | **1884** Fourteen nations attend Berlin Conference on West Africa and arbitrarily divide continent among themselves; France, Great Britain, Germany, and Portugal key players |
| | **1885** King Leopold II of Belgium becomes King of the Congo Free State; US first to recognize new monarchy |
| | **1886** Slavery abolished in Cuba |
| | **1886** Gold discovered in the Rand in Transvaal (South Africa) |
| **1887** National Colored Farmers' Alliance founded in Houston County, Texas | **1888** Abolition of slavery in Brazil |
| **1889** Ten thousand African Americans stake claims to land in newly opened Oklahoma | **1889** Sahle Mariam crowned Emperor of Ethiopia following death of Yohannes IV; he takes name Menelik II, signifying his descent from King Solomon and Queen of Sheba, whose son Menelik was first emperor of Ethiopia |
| **1890** Mississippi legislature approves new state constitution that effectively disfranchises all black voters | **1890** Italian and Ethiopian treaty translations found to differ; Ethiopia believes Italy has become its intermediary with foreign powers, but Italy believes Ethiopia is its protectorate |
| | **1890** Anglo-German agreement is reached regarding borders of Nigeria and Cameroon |
| **1892** First black college football game played, Biddle vs. Livingstone | **1892** German troops retreat from the Chagga near Moshi (Tanzania); more troops arrive to defeat the Chagga; the Hehe battle Germans at Kilosa (Tanzania) |
| **1892** *Afro-American Newspaper* founded by former slave John H. Murphy, Sr., in Baltimore | |
| **1894** Church of God in Christ founded in Memphis, Tennessee | **1894** Britain approves annexation of Swaziland by Transvaal (South Africa) |

*1895* Booker T. Washington delivers his "Atlanta Exposition Address":

> "In all things that are purely social we can be as separate as the fingers, yet one as the hand in all things essential to mutual progress."

*1895* Some 113 African Americans lynched in the South

*1895* National Baptist Convention USA organized in Atlanta, Georgia

*1896* US Supreme Court *Plessy v. Ferguson* decision sanctions "separate but equal" doctrine, paving way for more Jim Crow laws

*1897* American Negro Academy founded in Washington, DC to encourage African-American participation in art, literature, and philosophy, with Rev. Alexander Crummell as president

*1898* Louisiana legislature enacts Grandfather Clause, requiring that voter registration applicants be able to read and write; similar laws enacted in other Southern states limit black voter registration

*1898* African-American troops fight abroad for first time, in Spanish-American War

*1898* North Carolina Mutual Life Insurance Company founded by former slave John Merrick and associates in Durham, North Carolina

*1895* Cuban War of Independence; Afro-Cuban revolutionary hero Antonio Maceo appointed Lieutenant General of Cuban Liberation Army

*1895* Italy invades Ethiopia

*1896* Emperor Menelik II leads counterattack, defeating Italians at Adwa and recapturing Italian-held Eritrea

*1896* Asante territory refuses to become British protectorate; British send Asante king into exile

*1896* Afro-Portuguese writer Joaquim Maria Machado de Assis founding president of Brazilian Academy of Letters

*1897* In London, Samuel Coleridge-Taylor, son of Sierra Leone father and English mother, completes his most famous composition, *Hiawatha's Wedding Feast*

*1898* In Spanish-American War, the all-black US 9th and 10th Calvary units make possible Teddy Roosevelt's famous charge up San Juan Hill, in Cuba

*1898* In British conquest of Sudan, machine guns leave 11,000 Dervish soldiers dead and 16,000 wounded; British sustain only 48 casualties

*1898* Lagos, Nigeria, lit with electricity

| AFRICAN-AMERICAN | GLOBAL / AFRICAN DIASPORAN |
|---|---|
| *1899* Scott Joplin publishes "Maple Leaf Rag" | *1899* South African Boer War; Germany supplies Boers with armaments against British |
| | *1900* War of the Golden Stool, last Asante stand against incorporation into British Empire, led by Yaa Asantewa, an Asante noblewoman; the British exile Asantewa and other leaders |
| | *1900* First Pan-African Congress held in London; W. E. B. Du Bois leads US delegation |
| *1901* James Weldon Johnson, brother J. Rosamond Johnson, and Bob Cole first African Americans to sign songwriting contract for Broadway stage | *1901* Barred from many racing opportunities in southern US for racist reasons, African-American cyclist Marshall "Major" Taylor wins European Cycling championship in France |
| *1903* W. E. B. Du Bois publishes *The Souls of Black Folk*: | *1902 Off to Bloomingdale Asylum*, first French film using black actors, opens in Paris; black characters kick each other until they become white |

"The problem of the Twentieth Century is the problem of the color line."

| AFRICAN-AMERICAN | GLOBAL / AFRICAN DIASPORAN |
|---|---|
| *1903* African-American Maggie Lena Walker becomes first woman president of a local bank, founding St. Luke Penny Savings Bank in Richmond, Virginia | *1903* In Panama, thousands of black workers from surrounding nations and the Caribbean arrive in Canal Zone to begin construction of canal |
| *1903* Black cowboy Bill Pickett popularizes "bulldogging," method of steer wrestling that he invented | *1903* Britain completes conquest of northern Nigeria |
| | *1904* British report reveals Congo atrocities, including thousands mutilated and murdered by order of King Leopold II to gain profits from rubber |
| *1905 The Chicago Defender* begins publishing as champion of African-American rights | *1905* The Maji Maji revolt against German colonialism erupts in Tanganyika (Tanzania) |

*1905* Mark Twain supports first international human rights movement of 20th century, mobilized to end murderous reign of Leopold II in the Congo

*1906* Azuza Street Revival in Los Angeles inspires spread of Holiness, Pentecostal, and Apostolic churches

*1906* Madame C. J. Walker, African-American entrepreneur, launches prolific business career with hair-care company in Denver, Colorado

*1906* Alpha Phi Alpha, first college fraternity for black men, founded at Cornell University

*1907* Alain Locke arrives at Oxford University as first African-American Rhodes Scholar

*1907* Command performance of *In Dahomey*, starring black comedians Bert Williams and George Walker, given for King Edward VII in London

*1907* In South Africa, lawyer Mohandas Gandhi leads nonviolent protest against law mandating registration of all Indians

*1907* Picasso incorporates ceremonial masks of the Dogon tribe into his groundbreaking cubist work, *Les Demoiselles d'Avignon* (*The Young Ladies of Avignon*)

*1908* Alpha Kappa Alpha, first black women's sorority, founded at Howard University

*1908* Under pressure from Britain and US, Leopold II sells the Congo Free State to the Belgian government

*1908* Jack Johnson becomes first African-American world heavyweight champion

*1909* National Association for the Advancement of Colored People (NAACP) organized in New York City

*1909* Coup led by British officer to topple government of Liberian President Barclay fails

*1909* African-American Matthew Henson and Admiral Robert E. Peary, accompanied by four Inuit (Eskimos), believed to be first to reach the North Pole

*1909* *The Amsterdam News* begins publishing in New York City

*1910* US black population 9,827,763 (10.7 percent)

*1911* National Urban League founded in New York City

*1911* Kappa Alpha Psi fraternity founded at Indiana University and Omega Psi Phi at Howard University

*1912* W. C. Handy publishes "Memphis Blues" sheet music

*1913* Noble Drew Ali founds Moorish Science Temple in Newark, New Jersey

*1914* African-American inventor Garrett Morgan patents gas mask

*1914* Marcus Garvey founds Universal Negro Improvement Association, Conservation Association, and African Communities League (UNIA-ACL) in Kingston, Jamaica

*1914* Jack Johnson wins 20-round referee's decision over Frank Moran in Paris to retain his heavyweight title

*1915* US invades Haiti

*1910* Union of South Africa formed, uniting British colonies of Cape and Natal with Boer republics of Transvaal and Orange Free State; Louis Botha named prime minister

*1911* Sun Yat-sen persuades Ch'en Yu-jen (Eugene Chen), an Afro-Chinese lawyer from Trinidad, to leave London to join anti-imperialist movement in China

*1912* In Haiti, an explosion at National Palace kills President Cincinnatus Leconte and 300 soldiers; Gen. Tancrède Auguste succeeds him

*1913* Natives Land Act of South Africa leaves majority of blacks without land

*1913* German anthropologist Eugen Fischer publishes *Die Rehobother Bastards und das Bastardierungsproblem beim Menschen (The Rehoboth Bastards and the Problem of Cross-breeding in Man)*, his field research on race cross-breeding in German colony of South West Africa (today, Namibia), and calls for prohibition of mixed marriages within colonies

*1914* First World War erupts in late June; by August, many major clashes involve British, French, and German colonial forces in Africa

*1915* Carter G. Woodson founds Association for the Study of Negro Life and History

*1915* Ku Klux Klan revived in Atlanta, Georgia; by 1919 it has spread to 27 states

*1916* First issue of *Journal of Negro History,* edited by Carter G. Woodson, is published

*1916* American Tennis Association created to promote tennis among African Americans

## WAR, RENAISSANCE, AND DEPRESSION

*1917* US declares war on Germany in April; Congress passes Selective Service Act, calling for segregation of white and black soldiers in WWI; black troops are noncombat as US Army refuses to allow armed black soldiers among its ranks

*1917* US enters WWI; approximately 400,000 African Americans serve in armed forces

*1917* France accepts African-American combat infantry soldiers to fight under its flag after rejections from US and Britain, while 500,000 colonial Africans fight for British, French, and Germans

*1917* Ten to fifteen thousand blacks protest race riot in East St. Louis, Missouri, with silent march down New York's Fifth Avenue

*1918* James Reese Europe's all-black army band popularizes jazz in Europe

*1918* In last battle of WWI, 150 Germans and 3,000 Africans who had been unbeaten in four years surrender to British in Rhodesia (Zambia)

*1919* Ten thousand African-American noncombat soldiers are last US troops to leave France, as they remain to build hospitals, dig graves for American cemetery at Romagne

*1919* German surrender terms include loss of all of its African territory

*1919* W. E. B. Du Bois organizes the Second Pan-African Congress in Paris, France

*1919* Twenty-five race riots take place throughout country as hundreds killed during "Red Summer"

*1919* Inspired by Red Summer, Harlem Renaissance poet Claude McKay writes poem "If We Must Die":

> "If we must die, let it not be like hogs / Hunted and penned in an inglorious spot."

*1919* Marcus Garvey organizes Black Star Line steamship company to link black communities in commerce

*1919* Oscar Micheaux releases first feature-length film by an African American, *The Homesteader*

*1920* Marcus Garvey holds first International Convention of Negro Peoples of the World at Madison Square Garden, New York City

*1920* Former heavyweight boxing champion Jack Johnson opens Club Deluxe in Harlem; gangster Owney Madden buys it in 1922, changing its name to Cotton Club

*1920* Germans protest presence of some 20,000 black soldiers (from French colonies of North and West Africa, Madagascar, and the West Indies) stationed as peacekeeping force on Rhine

*1921* Pace Phonograph Company establishes first African-American record label, Black Swan Records

*1921* Jesse Binga founds successful black-owned bank in Chicago

*1921* Bessie Coleman is awarded international license in France by the Fédération Aéronautique Internationale, becoming first African-American woman pilot

*1921* Second Pan-African Congress convenes in Brussels, Paris, and London; resolutions include an end to "unrestrained greed" of capitalism

*1921* *Menschliche Erblichkeitslehre und Rassenhygiene (Human Heredity Teaching and Racial Hygiene)* by Erwin Baur, Eugen Fischer, and Fritz Lenz published; becomes foundational work for Nazi attitudes about race

*1921* Exhibition of African-American artists, including Henry Ossawa Tanner and Meta Warrick Fuller, at 135th Street branch of New York Public Library

*1921* Eubie Blake and Nobel Sissle's *Shuffle Along* first musical comedy by African Americans on Broadway

*1922* Black Star Line bankrupt: Garvey and associates indicted for mail fraud by J. Edgar Hoover

*1922* Senegalese boxer Louis Phal, aka Battling Siki, knocks out Georges Carpentier in Paris for world light-heavyweight boxing crown, becoming first African sports titlist

*1922* William Leo Hansberry of Howard University offers first African Studies course at an American university

*1922* Egypt receives nominal independence from Britain, nation's first semblance of self-rule since 323 BCE

*1922* Thirty Harlem Renaissance writers publish works: Claude McKay, Langston Hughes, Jean Toomer, Countee Cullen, James Weldon Johnson, Jesse Redmon Fauset, and Nella Larson, among others

*1923* Paul Revere Williams first African-American member of American Institute of Architects

*1923* Convening in London and Lisbon, Third Pan-African Congress demands that Africa be "for the benefit of Africans, and not merely for the profit of Europeans"

*1923* Bessie Smith, "Empress of the Blues," records hit song "Down-Hearted Blues"

*1923* Rosewood, black Florida town, destroyed by white mob from nearby towns

*1923* Garrett T. Morgan patents traffic signal

*1923* Bessie Smith's "Down-Hearted Blues/Gulf Coast Blues" first million-selling record by a black artist

*1923* National Urban League begins publishing *Opportunity* magazine

*1924* Immigration Act limits number of blacks who can migrate to US

*1924* Liberian government expels UNIA emissaries sent by Marcus Garvey

*1925* A. Philip Randolph founds Brotherhood of Sleeping Car Porters

*1925* Clifton Reginald Wharton first African American to enter US Foreign Service

*1925* Marcus Garvey, in Atlanta Federal Penitentiary, writes editorial for *Negro World:*

*1925* In *Mein Kampf,* Adolf Hitler proclaims Aryan race superior to all others

*1925* Tomb of Egyptian pharaoh Tutankhamen unearthed; some scholars seek to prove that Tutankhamen and other pharaohs were black

"There is no height to which we cannot climb by using the active intelligence of our own minds."

*1925* Ma Rainey, "Mother of the Blues," records "See See Rider"

*1925* Alain Locke compiles special edition of *Survey Graphic* magazine, acknowledging African roots of black art and music and emphasizing young generation of writers driving the Harlem Renaissance:

*1925* Josephine Baker thrills Paris audiences in *La Revue Negre*

"Youth speaks, and the voice of the New Negro is heard."

*1925* Alain Locke's *The New Negro* published in book form, featuring essay "The Negro Digs Up His Past" by Arthur Schomburg:

"The American Negro must remake his past in order to make his future."

*1926* Negro History Week celebrated for first time (becomes Black History Month in 1976)

*1926* New York Public Library acquires personal collection of Arturo (Arthur) Alfonso Schomburg, establishing foundation for Schomburg Center for Research in Black Culture

*1926* Langston Hughes publishes first collection of poetry, *The Weary Blues*

*1927* Marcus Garvey deported from US

*1926* League of Nation's Commission on Slavery declares labor system in cotton industry of American South "virtual slavery"

| AFRICAN-AMERICAN | GLOBAL/AFRICAN DIASPORAN |
|---|---|
| *1927* Harmon Foundation begins to promote African-American visual artists | *1927* In New York, Fourth Pan-African Congress calls for withdrawal of US Marines from Haiti |
| *1928* Oscar DePriest of Chicago first black elected to Congress since Reconstruction | |
| *1929* Collapse of US stock market leads to Great Depression | *1929* In India, Mohandas "Mahatma" Gandhi sends statement of solidarity to W.E.B. Du Bois, "Message to the American Negro" |
| *1929* Augusta Savage creates award-winning sculpture *Gamin* | |
| *1929* *Chicago Defender* circulation reaches 250,000 | *1929* Sixth UNIA International Convention convenes in Jamaica; 1,200 delegates from US, Africa, and West Indies attend |
| *1930* African-American population reaches 11,891,143 (9.7 percent) | *1930* Ras Tafari crowned Emperor Haile Selassie of Ethiopia |
| *1930* Wallace Fard Muhammad founds Nation of Islam in Detroit, Michigan | |
| *1930* James Weldon Johnson publishes *Black Manhattan* | |
| *1932* US Public Health Service starts Tuskegee Syphilis Experiment (lasts until 1972) | |
| *1932* Col. Leon H. Washington founds *Los Angeles Sentinel* newspaper | *1933* In Germany, Adolf Hitler's National Socialist German Workers (Nazi) Party comes into power; Nazi law legalizes forced sterilization of handicapped persons, Gypsies, blacks, and persons of mixed race |
| | *1933* At Tokyo luncheon, author Langston Hughes declares Japanese are model for "dark people in the world" |
| *1934* Elijah Muhammad assumes control of Nation of Islam and moves headquarters to Chicago | *1934* German officials discourage touring African-American entertainers, deeming jazz immoral, decadent, excessively erotic, and promulgated by Jews |
| *1934* Zora Neal Hurston publishes first novel, *Jonah's Gourd Vine:* | |

"No one pushed him uphill, but everyone was willing to lend a hand on the downward shove."

*1934* Apollo Theater opens in Harlem

# WORLD WAR II AND THE CIVIL RIGHTS STRUGGLE

*1935* Mary McLeod Bethune unites 28 national women's organizations to create National Council of Negro Women:

*1935* Italian army, under leadership of Benito Mussolini, invades Ethiopia

"The true worth of a race must be measured by the character of its womanhood."

—BETHUNE'S SPEECH TO CHICAGO WOMEN'S FEDERATION, 1933

*1935* Interracial Southern Tenant Farmers' Union organizes multistate strike of cotton pickers for better wages

*1935* Marcus Garvey moves UNIA headquarters from Jamaica to London

*1936* National Negro Congress of nearly 600 black organizations meets in Chicago

*1936* Civil War erupts in Spain; 3,200 Americans join antifascist cause, including several African Americans

*1936* Mary McLeod Bethune named Director of Division of Negro Affairs, National Youth Administration, by Franklin D. Roosevelt, first black woman to receive presidential appointment

*1936* Mary McLeod Bethune regularly convenes black colleagues in federal positions and civil rights leaders (the Black Cabinet) to discuss ways to increase federal services to blacks and improve living standards for black communities

*1936* Track star Jesse Owens wins four gold medals at Berlin Olympics, debunking Hitler's racial superiority myth

*1936* Delta blues musician Robert Johnson records "Crossroad Blues," one of only 29 songs he recorded

*1937* Joe Louis wins heavyweight championship, defeating James J. Braddock in Chicago

*1937* Katherine Dunham forms Negro Dance Group to present African, African-American, and African diasporan dance forms

*1937* Southern Negro Youth Congress organized to fight for political, social, and economic justice

*1937* Actor and singer Paul Robeson addresses antifascist Spanish Civil War Rally in London:

"The artist must elect to fight for freedom or for slavery. I have made my choice. I have no alternative."

*1938* Joe Louis beats Max Schmeling in rematch following his 1936 defeat by German boxer

*1938* Jacob Lawrence completes *Toussaint L'Overture* series and holds first solo exhibition at Harlem YMCA

*1938* Folk artist Horace Pippin included in "Masters of Popular Painting" exhibition at Museum of Modern Art, New York

*1938* An exhibition in Düsseldorf entitled "Entartete Musik"("Degenerate Music") condemns African-American jazz and music by Jewish composers as degenerate, along with artists who perform it

*1939* Marian Anderson performs before 75,000 at Lincoln Memorial after Daughters of American Revolution refuse to permit performance at Constitution Hall

*1939* Germany invades Poland on September 1, beginning World War II

*1939* Jazz singer Billie Holiday popularizes antilynching anthem "Strange Fruit":

"Southern trees bear strange fruit / Blood on the leaves and blood at the root."

*1939* Jane Bolin first African-American woman judge in US

*1940* NAACP establishes Legal Defense and Educational Fund to wage legal struggle against segregation

*1940–43* Allies fight Germans and Italians in Africa campaigns fought in West, East, and North Africa; both Allied and Axis armies include Africans troops

**1940** Richard Wright publishes first novel, *Native Son*

**1940** Dr. Charles Drew develops first blood bank after discovering that plasma can replace whole blood transfusions; directs Blood for Britain project in war-ravaged London

**1940** Benjamin O. Davis first African-American general in US Army

**1940** Hattie McDaniel, first black actor to win an Academy Award, presented Oscar for Best Supporting Actress role in *Gone with the Wind*

**1941** Rev. Adam Clayton Powell Jr. leads successful four-week bus boycott in Harlem to secure black drivers and mechanics and wins job concessions from other companies:

**1940** Félix Eboué, French Guianese-born governor of Chad, first colonial French leader to support Free French army of Charles de Gaulle

**1941** Gideon Force, a cadre of British, Sudanese, and Ethiopian troops, assists Allies in several successful operations against Italians in East Africa

"Use what you have right in your hand. That dollar . . . that ten cents. Use your vote. The Negro race has enough power right in our hands to accomplish anything we want to."

**1941** Japanese bomb Pearl Harbor; US enters World War II; African-American labor and communication units among first US soldiers deployed

**1941** A. Philip Randolph calls for March on Washington to end discrimination in US defense industries

**1941** President Franklin D. Roosevelt issues Executive Order 8802, establishing Fair Employment Practices Committee (FEPC) to prevent racial discrimination in defense plants

**1941** First class of Tuskegee Airmen, unit of black combat pilots, begins training; by war's end, Tuskegee Airmen would destroy or damage more than 400 enemy planes without losing one of their bombers

**1941** Haile Selassie restored to throne in Ethiopia

*1942–43* One hundred thousand African-American noncombat soldiers sent to Alaska, Asia, and Pacific to build roads, ports, and airfields for campaigns at Midway, Coral Sea, and Guadalcanal

*1942* Jacob Lawrence's landmark *Migration Series* of paintings purchased by Museum of Modern Art and Phillips Collection

*1942* Congress of Racial Equality (CORE) founded in Chicago

*1942* First African Americans admitted to US Marine Corps

*1943* Annapolis and other naval officer schools enroll first African Americans

*1943* President Roosevelt goes to Liberia seeking rubber for war effort

*1944* Some 1,800 African-American soldiers part of Normandy D-Day assault

*1944* Army Transportation Corps launches Red Ball Express; nearly 75 percent of supply truck drivers African American

*1944* US Supreme Court declares "white only" political primaries unconstitutional

*1944* Frederick Douglass Patterson establishes United Negro College Fund to support black colleges and students

*1944* Adam Clayton Powell Jr. elected to Congress, representing Harlem

*1944* Thelonius Monk records jazz standard "'Round Midnight"

*1945* WWII victory against Germany and Japan declared; more than one million black men and 4,000 black women served during war, and over one million colonial African troops served with Allied forces

*1942* Robertsfield Airport in Liberia built during WWII for B47 bombers to refuel, creating longest runway in Africa at the time

*1942* In response to bombing of Pearl Harbor, Caribbean Defense Command increases troops from 60,000 in November 1941 to 119,000 in December 1942, more than half of whom are in Panama guarding the Canal

*1943* African troops join British and Americans in Allied invasion of Italy

*1944–45* The 81st and 82nd West African Divisions and 11th East African Division fight Japanese in Burma

*1944* Eliud Mathu first black member of legislative council in Kenya

*1945* World War II ends with German, then Japanese, surrender

*1945* John H. Johnson publishes first issue of *Ebony* magazine

*1945* Nat King Cole first African American to host radio variety show

*1945* Saxophonist Charlie "Bird" Parker records seminal bebop song "Koko" with trumpeters Miles Davis and John Birks "Dizzy" Gillespie

*1946* US Supreme Court rules segregation in interstate bus travel to be unconstitutional

*1946* President Harry S. Truman establishes President's Committee on Civil Rights to investigate racial injustice and make recommendations

*1947* Jackie Robinson joins Brooklyn Dodgers as first African American to play Major League Baseball in 20th century

*1947* NAACP's "An Appeal to the World" petitions United Nations to end racism in US

*1947* Tuskegee Institute report finds 3,432 African Americans lynched since 1882

*1947* CORE organizes Journey of Reconciliation, an interracial bus trip through South to test Supreme Court ruling banning segregation in interstate bus travel

*1948* President Truman issues Executive Order #9981, ordering desegregation of armed forces

*1948* California Supreme Court voids law banning interracial marriage

*1948* "Dixiecrats" form States' Rights Democratic Party; nominate South Carolina Governor Strom Thurmond for President

*1945* "Freedom Now" is theme of Fifth Pan-African Congress in England, with attendees Jomo Kenyatta of Kenya and Kwame Nkrumah of Ghana

*1946* Australia sponsors massive postwar immigration program, inviting "whites only" and only fair-complexion émigrés from Italy, Spain, Portugal, Greece, and Turkey

*1947* British Crown colony of India replaced by independent nations of India and Pakistan

*1947* In South Africa, African National Congress forms an alliance with Natal Indian Congress and Transvaal Indian Congress

*1947* *Presence Africaine*, journal devoted to African culture, established by Alioine Diop in Senegal

*1948* South African prime minister Daniel Malan implements apartheid (apartness) to preserve white rule by legislating a racially separate and unequal nation

*1948* Israel declared independent, then attacked by surrounding Arab nations; United Nations dispatches mediators Count Folke Bernadotte and African American Ralph Bunche

*1948* Atlanta Police Department hires first black officers

*1948* NAACP President D. V. Carter beaten by whites in Montgomery, Alabama, for bringing black citizens to polls to vote

*1948* Muddy Waters releases blues classic "Rollin' Stone"

*1949* African American Ralph Bunche, named United Nations' chief mediator after assassination of Bernadotte, brokers armistice between Israel and five Arab states

*1949* North Atlantic Treaty Organization (NATO) established

*1949* People's Republic of China established

*1949* WERD-AM, first black-owned radio station, begins broadcasting from Atlanta

*1949* US armed forces create policy of equal treatment and opportunity for African Americans

*1950* African-American population reaches 15,042,286

*1950* Gwendolyn Brooks first African American to receive Pulitzer Prize, winning for poetry

*1950* Ralph Bunche first African-American recipient of Nobel Peace Prize for mediating settlement between Arabs and Israelis in 1948 conflict

*1950* Thurgood Marshall and NAACP challenge school segregation in Clarendon County, South Carolina

*1950* US Supreme Court rules that blacks have right to attend white graduate schools, receiving full academic benefits

*1950* Juanita Hall first African American to win Tony for her role in *South Pacific*

*1950–1953* More than 600,000 African Americans serve in the Korean War

*1951* Illinois National Guard called out to protect black family from mob of more than 3,000 whites trying to prevent them from moving into Cicero, Illinois, apartment

*1951* Jomo Kenyatta, president of Kenya African Union, campaigns for return of land taken by white settlers

*1951* New York City bans racial discrimination in public housing

*1951* *Brown v. Board of Education* filed in US District Court, Kansas, challenging school segregation

*1951* Johnson Publishing Company publishes first issue of *Jet,* weekly news magazine of black America

*1951* President Truman establishes committee to enforce nondiscriminatory practices in businesses with government contracts

*1951* Harry T. Moore, Florida NAACP official, and his wife killed by bomb in Mims, Florida

*1952* Ralph Ellison's *Invisible Man* is published:

"I am invisible, understand, simply because people refuse to see me."

*1952* Mau Mau Revolt erupts in Kenya; British imprison Jomo Kenyatta, declaring him responsible for event, which he denies

*1952* Fulgencio Batista, former de facto military leader (1933–40) and president (1940–44) of Cuba, stages a coup d'état, establishing a new dictatorship

*1953* Benjamin O. Davis Jr. becomes commander of 51st Fighter Interceptor Wing in Korea

*1953* Fidel Castro leads unsuccessful attack against Batista's forces in Moncada barracks

*1953* African Americans in Baton Rouge, Louisiana, begin boycott of city's segregated bus line

*1953* Hulan Jack elected first African-American president of New York's Borough of Manhattan

*1953* Willie Thrower becomes first black NFL quarterback in modern era, playing for the Chicago Bears

*1954* US Supreme Court ruling in *Brown v. Board of Education* declares segregation in nation's public schools unconstitutional

*1954* Benjamin O. Davis Jr. first black Air Force general and first black to command an airbase

*1954* Malcolm X becomes minister of Nation of Islam's Temple No. 7 in Harlem

*1954* Citizens of Jackson, Mississippi, vote to continue segregation

*1954* Dorothy Dandridge, star of *Carmen Jones,* first African-American actress nominated for Academy Award in best actress category

*1955* Emmett Till, 14-year-old Chicagoan, lynched in Money, Mississippi

*1955* Rosa Parks refuses to give up bus seat to white man, sparking 381-day Montgomery Bus Boycott in Alabama

*1955* Rev. Martin Luther King Jr., 26-year-old pastor of Dexter Avenue Baptist Church, elected president of Montgomery Improvement Association and becomes leader of bus boycott

*1955* NAACP wins court order prohibiting University of Alabama from denying Autherine Lucy admission to graduate school; she enters but is expelled

*1954* In Tanganyika (present-day Tanzania), Julius Nyerere resigns from teaching in order to tour country and gain support for independence without war or bloodshed

*1955* Bandung Conference between leaders of African and Asian countries held in Indonesia

*1955* Federal Interstate Commerce Commission bans segregation on interstate trains and buses

*1955* Chess Records releases Chuck Berry's hit record *Maybellene*

*1956* Nat King Cole becomes first African American to host prime-time television variety show

*1956* Harry Belafonte's *Calypso* first album in history to sell more than one million copies

*1956* Bombing of home of Martin Luther King Jr.

*1956* Alabama state legislature asks Congress for funds to relocate Alabama African Americans to cities in North and Midwest

*1956* Rev. Fred Shuttlesworth founds Alabama Christian Movement for Human Rights in Birmingham to replace banned NAACP in May; home bombed later that year but he is not hurt:

*1956* Eric Williams founds People's National Movement in Trinidad

*1956* First International Congress of Black Writers and Artists held in Paris

**"They can outlaw an organization [NAACP], but they cannot outlaw the movement of a people determined to be free."**

*1956* US Supreme Court declares bus segregation unconstitutional

*1956* Mississippi Sovereignty Commission formed to maintain racial segregation

*1956* Tanks deployed against whites protesting high school integration in Clinton, Tennessee

*1957* E. Franklin Frazier publishes *Black Bourgeoisie,* criticizing complacent black middle class

*1957* Civil Rights Act of 1957 establishes Civil Rights Division of Justice Department and US Commission on Civil Rights

*1957* *Black Orpheus,* journal of African writing, founded in Nigeria

*1957* Ghana achieves independence, marking beginning of postcolonial era for Africa and the Caribbean

*1957* François Duvalier elected president of Haiti, writes new constitution

*1957* Dorothy Height appointed president of National Council of Negro Women

*1957* Althea Gibson becomes first African American to win Women's Singles at Wimbledon tennis tournament

*1957* Marian Anderson sings National Anthem at inauguration of President Dwight D. Eisenhower

*1957* "Little Rock Nine" admitted to Central High School after President Eisenhower sends federal troops to enforce desegregation

*1958* Southern Christian Leadership Conference (SCLC) organized in Atlanta with Martin Luther King Jr. as president

*1958* Nigerian Chinua Achebe publishes *Things Fall Apart,* an examination of Western civilization and its threat to traditional African values

*1958* Alvin Ailey American Dance Theater organized in New York City

*1958* White Afrikaners officially gain independence from Great Britain in South Africa

*1958* Martin Luther King Jr. stabbed in Harlem department store during book signing for *Stride Toward Freedom*

*1958* Little Rock citizens vote against integration of public schools

*1958* Edson Arantes do Nascimento, 17-year-old prodigy known to world as Pelé, leads Brazilian National Soccer team to its first ever World Cup championship in Sweden

*1959* 10,000 students participate in Youth March for Integrated Schools in Washington, DC

*1959* Fidel Castro comes to power in Cuba

*1959* Lorraine Hansberry's *A Raisin in the Sun* opens on Broadway:

*1959* South African writer Es'kia Mphahlele's classic autobiography *Down Second Avenue* published

> "Son—I come from five generations of people who was slaves and sharecroppers—but ain't nobody in my family never let nobody pay 'em no money that was a way of telling us we wasn't fit to walk the earth."

*1959* CORE organizes nonviolent sit-ins in Miami

*1959* National symphony orchestra of Ghana founded

*1959* Miles Davis begins recording album *Kind of Blue*

*1959* Ella Fitzgerald and William "Count" Basie first African-American Grammy winners

*1959* Sam Cooke founds SAR Records, one of first independent music labels founded by an African American

*1960* African-American population 18,871,831 (10.6 percent)

*1960* Students from North Carolina A&T College in Greensboro, North Carolina, hold sit-in at Woolworth's to desegregate lunch counters

*1960* Student Nonviolent Coordinating Committee (SNCC) founded under leadership of civil rights leader Ella Baker:

*1960* South African Albert John Lutuli, President of the African National Congress, wins Nobel Peace Prize

*1960* Congo gains independence from Belgium, and war erupts; Prime Minister Patrice Lumumba aided by Soviet Union against President Joseph Kasavubu and Col. Joseph Mobutu

## "Give light and people will find the way."

*1960* Track star Wilma Rudolph of Tennessee State University wins three gold medals at Olympics in Rome

*1960* Abebe Bikila, barefoot Ethiopian runner, becomes first African to win Olympic gold medal

*1960* South African police end peaceful anti-apartheid demonstration in Sharpeville, killing 69 and wounding nearly 200 men, women, and children

*1961* CORE organizes Freedom Rides through the Deep South

*1961* African-American students Charlayne Hunter (later known as Charlayne Hunter-Gault) and Hamilton Holmes enroll at University of Georgia despite riots to stop them

*1961* Congressman Adam Clayton Powell Jr. becomes chairman of House Education and Labor Committee, authors "war on poverty" bills

*1961* Robert C. Weaver becomes administrator of US Housing and Home Finance Agency, highest federal position held by an African American

*1961* Belgian mercenaries kidnap Congolese prime minister Lumumba, who is then killed by Moise Tshombe's troops

*1961* Dominican Republic dictator Rafael Trujillo assassinated

*1961* Failed Bay of Pigs invasion of Cuba embarrasses US

*1961* Elections spur racial violence in British Guiana

*1961* Tanganyika achieves independence, with Julius Nyerere as prime minister

*1961* SNCC Freedom Riders travel to Montgomery, Birmingham, and Anniston, Alabama; New Orleans, Louisiana; and Jackson, Mississippi, to test Supreme Court interstate bus travel decision

*1961* After nine years in prison, Jomo Kenyatta formally elected president of Kenya African National Union. He had been elected president in absentia in 1960

*1961* In South Africa, the ANC (African National Congress) begins to covertly organize an armed struggle

*1962* Council of Federated Organizations (COFO) formed to coordinate civil rights struggles in Mississippi

*1962* NAACP sues Rochester, New York, school system for de facto segregation

*1962* Jackie Robinson first African American inducted into Baseball Hall of Fame

*1962* Over 23,000 soldiers federalized by President John F. Kennedy to ensure enrollment of James Meredith at University of Mississippi

*1962* Nelson Mandela leaves South Africa illegally to address Conference of the Pan-African Freedom Movement of East and Central Africa in Ethiopia

*1962* Conviction on leaving South Africa illegally and sabotage gets Mandela sentenced to life imprisonment on Robben Island

*1962* Twenty-one-member Organization of American States (OAS) votes to exclude Cuba from membership

*1962* Jamaica and Trinidad and Tobago become independent

*1962* Brazil rules in soccer, and Pelé is rated best player in world; Brazil wins World Cup despite Pelé's withdrawal from tournament due to injury

*1963* Martin Luther King Jr. writes "Letter from a Birmingham Jail" in response to article by eight white Alabama clergymen protesting his presence in city:

*1963* Kenya achieves independence; Jomo Kenyatta elected prime minister

"Injustice anywhere is a threat to justice everywhere."

*1963* Mississippi NAACP Field Secretary Medgar Evers murdered in front of his home in Jackson

*1963* Over 250,000 people attend March on Washington where Martin Luther King Jr. delivers "I Have a Dream" speech

*1963* United Nations (and Tshombe) recognize confederated Congo government of President Kasavubu and Army commander-in-chief General Mobutu (backed by US)

*1963* First conference of Organization of African Unity held in Addis Ababa

*1963* Despite federal court ruling barring state government interference, Governor George Wallace stands in University of Alabama doorway blocking admission of Vivian Malone and James Hood

*1963* Four African-American girls, ages 11 to 14, killed in KKK bombing of 16th Street Baptist Church in Birmingham, Alabama

*1963* President John F. Kennedy is assassinated

*1963* Malcolm X addresses Northern Negro Grass Roots Leadership Conference, Detroit, Michigan:

**"If violence is wrong in America, violence is wrong abroad."**

*1964* President Lyndon B. Johnson declares an "unconditional war on poverty in America"

*1964* Sidney Poitier first black actor to win an Academy Award in best actor category for his role in 1963 film *Lilies of the Field*

*1964* COFO sponsors Mississippi Freedom Summer Project; participants Michael Schwerner, Andrew Goodman, and James Chaney are murdered in Neshoba County, Mississippi

*1964* Mississippi Freedom Democratic Party (MFDP) denied seats at Democratic National Convention in Atlantic City, New Jersey

*1964* Coup in Zanzibar topples Jamshid bin Abdullah; Zanzibar joins with Tanganyika to form new nation, Tanzania, with Julius Nyerere as president

*1964* Abebe Bikila becomes first two-time gold medalist in Olympic marathon

*1964* Kenyan Ngugi wa Thiong'o's novel *Weep Not, Child* first major novel in English by an East African

*1964* Fannie Lou Hamer, MFDP Vice Chair and SNCC worker, testifies at Democratic Convention's Credentials Committee about beatings and threats for attempting to register to vote in Mississippi:

> "Is this America, the land of the free and the home of the brave . . . ?"

*1964* Civil Rights Act of 1964 bans discrimination in public accommodations and establishes the Equal Employment Opportunity Commission (EEOC)

*1964* Martin Luther King Jr. awarded Nobel Peace Prize in Stockholm, Sweden

*1964* At 63 years of age, Louis Armstrong records Grammy-winning *Hello Dolly,* knocks Beatles off Billboard Top 100 chart to become number one pop song

# FROM BLACK POWER TO THE NEW MILLENNIUM

*1965* Malcolm X assassinated at Audubon Ballroom in Harlem

*1965* Selma to Montgomery marchers eventually number 25,000 when they reach Alabama capitol on their second try

*1965* Watts uprising in Los Angeles, California, leaves 34 dead and 1,000 injured

*1965* Robert C. Weaver, named Secretary of Housing and Urban Development, becomes first African-American cabinet member

*1965* Hit single *I Got You (I Feel Good)* by James Brown, "The Godfather of Soul," released

*1966* Black Panther Party formed in Oakland, California, by Huey P. Newton and Bobby Seal

*1965* Joseph Mobuto stages US-backed coup, taking over Congolese presidency

*1965* US invasion to quell political unrest in Dominican Republic ends with Act of Dominican Reconciliation, setting up temporary government until national elections in 1966

*1965* Argentine-born Cuban revolutionary Ernesto "Che" Guevara arrives in Kimbamba to help Congolese rebels

*1966* Barbados and British Guiana (now Guyana) achieve independence

*1966* Edward Brooke of Massachusetts becomes first African American popularly elected to US Senate

*1966* Stokely Carmichael succeeds John Lewis as head of SNCC, advocates "Black Power"

*1966* Jazz legend Edward Kennedy "Duke" Ellington awarded Grammy Lifetime Achievement Award; awarded Presidential Medal of Freedom three years later

*1966* California professor Maulana Karenga creates Kwanzaa

*1967* Martin Luther King Jr. delivers "Beyond Vietnam" speech at Riverside Church in New York City:

*1966* First World Festival of Negro Arts (FESTAC) held in Dakar, Senegal

*1966* *Efuru*, by Nigerian Flora Nwapa, one of first published English-language novels by an African woman

"If we do not act we shall surely be dragged down the long dark and shameful corridors of time reserved for those who possess power without compassion, might without morality, and strength without sight."

*1967* Newark riots result in 26 dead, 1,500 injured, 1,000 arrested

*1967* President Lyndon Johnson appoints Thurgood Marshall first African-American Supreme Court Justice

*1968* Three South Carolina State College students killed and 27 wounded by police in Orangeburg Massacre after their attempt to desegregate bowling alley

*1968* Martin Luther King Jr. assassinated in Memphis, Tennessee

*1968* Coretta Scott King establishes Martin Luther King, Jr. Center for Social Change (now The King Center) in Atlanta

*1967* Trinidad and Tobago, and Barbados join the OAS

*1968* Caribbean Free Trade Area formed

*1968* Noted Senegalese writer and film director Ousmane Sembène creates *Mandabi,* first film in native Wolof language

*1968* Congressman John Conyers of Michigan introduces bill to establish national holiday honoring Martin Luther King Jr.

*1968* Uprisings occur in 125 cities across 29 states

*1968* Poor People's Campaign brings over 50,000 demonstrators to Washington, DC, to protest poverty in US

*1968* Civil Rights Act of 1968 outlaws discrimination in housing sales and rentals

*1968* Shirley Chisholm first black woman elected to US Congress

*1968* Arthur Ashe becomes first African American to win Men's Singles in US Open Tennis competition

*1969* Moneta Sleet Jr. of *Ebony* magazine wins Pulitzer Prize in Photography

*1969* Jamaica joins OAS; border clashes between Guyana and Surinam; riots in Curaçao

*1969* Alfred Day Hershey shares Nobel Prize in Medicine for work on replication and genetic structure of viruses

*1969* Jimi Hendrix headlines Woodstock Festival

*1969* James Earl Jones wins his first Tony for his role in *The Great White Hope*

*1970* Clifton Wharton Jr. becomes first African American to head predominantly white university when he is selected as president of Michigan State University

*1970* Guyana becomes republic

*1970* Black Power movement in Trinidad challenges leadership of Eric Williams

*1970* African-American population reaches 22,580,289 (11.1 percent)

*1970* Brazil's largely Afro-Brazilian team becomes first to win World Cup three times; awarded Jules Rimet Trophy permanently

*1970* Toni Morrison publishes first novel, *The Bluest Eye*

*1970* Ed Lewis and Clarence O. Smith publish first issue of *Essence* magazine

*1970* Earl G. Graves publishes first edition of *Black Enterprise* magazine

*1970* Charles Gordone becomes first African American to win Pulitzer Prize in Drama for *No Place to Be Somebody*

*1970* Joint Center for Political and Economic Studies founded in Washington, DC, to provide training and technical assistance to newly elected black officials

*1971* Rev. Jesse Jackson founds People United to Save Humanity (PUSH) in Chicago, Illinois

*1971* Whitney Museum of American Art presents major exhibition of 20th-century black artists

*1971* Romare Bearden, black collage artist, has solo art exhibition at Museum of Modern Art in New York City

*1971* Johnson Products becomes first black-owned company listed on major US stock exchange (AMEX)

*1971* Leroy "Satchel" Paige first former Negro League baseball player inducted into Baseball Hall of Fame

*1971* Congressional Black Caucus founded in Washington, DC

*1972* Gary, Indiana, hosts National Black Political Convention; 8,000 delegates adopt Black Agenda and oppose school integration

*1972* Congresswoman Shirley Chisholm becomes first African-American woman to run for US presidency

*1972* Texan Barbara Jordan and Georgian Andrew Young first black congressional representatives from the South in 20th century

*1972* First Haitian boat people arrive in South Florida

*1971* President Mobutu renames Democratic Republic of the Congo Zaire and requires citizens to Africanize their names and dress; he becomes Mobutu Sese Seko

*1971* Idi Amin deposes Milton Obote in military coup in Uganda

*1972* Malian director Souleymane Cissé releases first fiction film, *Cinq Jours d'une vie (Five Days in a Life)*

*1972* Wilt Chamberlain becomes first NBA player to score 30,000 points

*1973* Motown icon Diana Ross nominated for an Academy Award in Best Actress category for her role as Billie Holiday in *Lady Sings the Blues*

*1973* African Americans Tom Bradley, Maynard Jackson, and Coleman Young elected mayors of Los Angeles, Atlanta, and Detroit, respectively

*1973* Marian Wright Edelman founds Children's Defense Fund to advocate for underprivileged children

*1973* Eleanor Holmes Norton helps found National Black Feminist Organization

*1973* Fidel Castro takes two-month tour of Eastern Europe, Soviet Union, and Africa

*1973* Jamaica, Guyana, Trinidad and Tobago, and Barbados found the Caribbean Community and Common Market (CARICOM)

*1973* The Bahamas gain independence

*1974* Henry "Hank" Aaron hits 715th home run, becomes all-time leader in Major League Baseball

*1974* The Links, Inc., makes largest gift by black organization with donation of $132,000 to United Negro College Fund

*1974* Muhammad Ali regains World Heavyweight Championship by knocking out George Foreman in Kinshasa, Zaire:

*1974* Sixth Pan-African Congress convenes in Tanzania

*1974* Grenada gains independence

*1974* Ethiopian emperor Haile Selassie deposed in coup led by Teferi Benti

**"Now you see me, now you don't. George thinks he will, but I know he won't!"**

*1974* George Brown and Mervyn Dymally first elected black lieutenant governors in nation's history, representing Colorado and California, respectively

*1974* Stevie Wonder wins Grammy Award for album *Innervisions*

*1975* Frank Robinson becomes first African-American manager of Major League Baseball team when chosen to manage Cleveland Indians

*1975* Angola, though divided, receives independence from Portugal

*1975* Fidel Castro sends Cuban troops to Angola in response to South African invasion of that country

| AFRICAN-AMERICAN | GLOBAL/AFRICAN DIASPORAN |
|---|---|
| *1975* Lee Elder first black golfer to compete in Masters Tournament in Augusta, Georgia | *1975* OAS votes to end its 11-year boycott of Cuba and reestablish normal diplomatic relations |
| *1975* Arthur Ashe wins Men's Singles title at England's Wimbledon Championships | *1975* Surinam becomes independent |
| *1975* Wallace D. Muhammad assumes control of Nation of Islam after death of his father Elijah Muhammad and later changes his name to Warith | |
| *1975* WGPR-TV, first black-owned television station, begins broadcasting in Detroit, Michigan | |
| *1976* College and university enrollment of African Americans rises to 1,062,000 from 282,000 in 1966 | *1976* In Angola, fighting intensifies between Popular Movement for the Liberation of Angola (MPLA) and Union for the Total Independence of Angola (UNITA) |
| *1976* Janie L. Mines first African-American woman cadet to enter US Naval Academy at Annapolis, Maryland | |
| *1976* Congresswoman Barbara Jordan first African-American woman to deliver keynote address at Democratic National Convention: | |

**"For the American idea, though it is shared by all of us, is realized in each one of us."**

| | |
|---|---|
| *1976* Los Angeles County Museum presents exhibition "Two Centuries of Black American Art" | |
| *1977* Writer Alex Haley's bestseller *Roots* wins special Pulitzer Prize | *1977* Black Consciousness Movement founder Steve Biko brutally beaten in his jail cell in South Africa; dies next day of massive brain hemorrhage in prison hospital cell |
| *1977* Patricia Harris becomes first African-American woman cabinet member as Secretary of Housing and Urban Development | |
| *1977* Congressman Andrew Young appointed US Ambassador to United Nations by President Jimmy Carter | *1977* FESTAC '77, second World Black and African Festival of Art and Culture, held in Lagos, Nigeria |
| *1977* *Roots* television series breaks all previous television viewing records for dramatic series with viewership of 130 million | *1977* First Congress of Black Culture in the Americas convenes in Colombia, resolves to vindicate contributions of the people "of African origin in the continent" |

*1977* African-American activist Randall Robinson founds TransAfrica Forum, lobbying group for human rights in Africa and African diasporan communities across globe

*1978* Louis Farrakahn breaks with Wallace D. Muhammad's World Community of Islam and revives Nation of Islam

*1978* Muhammad Ali wins his third heavyweight boxing title, defeating Leon Spinks in New Orleans, Louisiana

*1979* Rap emerges as new music genre when "Rappers Delight" by Sugar Hill Gang becomes first top-40 rap single

*1979* Black professor Sir Arthur Lewis of Princeton University awarded Nobel Prize in Economics

*1979* Franklin Thomas appointed president of Ford Foundation, becoming first African American to head major philanthropic foundation

*1979* Hazel W. Johnson first African-American woman general in US Army

*1980* African-American population reaches 26,482,349 (11.7 percent)

*1980* Willie Lewis Brown Jr. becomes first African-American speaker in a state legislature, the California Assembly

*1980* Robert L. Johnson founds Black Entertainment Television (BET) in Washington, DC

*1980* Toni Cade Bambara's *The Salt Eaters* published; wins American Book Award the following year

*1977* Janelle Commissiong, representing Trinidad and Tobago, crowned Miss Universe, becoming first woman of African descent to win the title

*1978* Ethiopia defeats invasion by Somalia with massive Soviet and Cuban aid and nationalizes factories, banks, and insurance companies

*1979* Rhodesia's seven-year civil war ends; Prime Minister Ian Smith promises gradual transfer of power from 250,000 whites to the nation's 6.8 million blacks

*1979* Amin's brutal dictatorship ends; he flees to Libya

*1979* Sir Arthur Lewis of Princeton University (born in St. Lucia) shares Nobel Prize in economics with Theodore W. Schultz of University of Chicago

*1980* In Rhodesia's first-ever democratic elections, the black majority elects Robert Mugabe prime minister of newly named, independent Zimbabwe

*1980* Mariel boatlift transports 125,000 Cubans to Florida; many African Americans see US national policy as hypocritical, as Haitian refugees routinely returned or detained for long periods

*1980* Sgt. Samuel K. Doe leads successful coup in Liberia, installing himself as dictator

| AFRICAN-AMERICAN | GLOBAL/AFRICAN DIASPORAN |
|---|---|
| **1981** Important works published by Maya Angelou (*The Heart of a Woman*), Toni Morrison (*Tar Baby*), and David Bradley (*The Chaneysville Massacre*) | **1981** Belize, formerly British Honduras, becomes last British colony in mainland Americas to achieve independence |
| **1981** Broadway hits include *Dreamgirls, Sophisticated Ladies,* and *Lena Horne: The Lady and Her Music* | |
| **1981** Charles Fuller's *A Soldier's Play* wins New York Drama Critics' Circle Award and Pulitzer Prize following year | |
| **1982** Bryant Gumbel becomes first African-American anchor on major network, joining NBC's *Today Show* | **1982** Nelson Mandela transferred from Robbin Island to Pollsmoor Prison in Cape Town |
| **1982** Congress extends Voting Rights Act of 1965 for additional 25 years, making some sections permanent | |
| **1982** Quincy Jones wins five Grammy Awards for album *The Dude* | |
| **1982** Michael Jackson's album *Thriller* sells more than 45 million copies, becoming best-selling album in music history | |
| **1982** Painter Jean-Michel Basquiat has his first solo show at Annina Nosei Gallery in New York | |
| **1982** Rev. Ben Chavis launches national campaign against environmental racism when he and followers block siting of toxic waste dump in Warren County, North Carolina | |
| **1983** President Ronald Reagan signs bill establishing federal holiday on third Monday of every January, celebrating Martin Luther King Jr.'s birthday on January 15th | **1983** Assassination of Maurice Bishop, pro-Soviet prime minister of Grenada, followed by US military invasion of Grenada |
| **1983** Harold Washington elected first black mayor of Chicago | |
| **1983** Guion (Guy) S. Bluford becomes first African-American astronaut to make space flight as crew member on *Challenger* | |

*1983* Alice Walker's *The Color Purple* wins Pulitzer Prize for Fiction and National Book Award

*1984* W. Wilson Goode becomes the first African-American mayor of Philadelphia

*1984* Prince's soundtrack album for his movie *Purple Rain* released, goes on to sell 13 million copies worldwide

*1984* Rev. Jesse Jackson wins almost one fourth of votes cast in Democratic primaries and caucuses and one eighth of convention delegates in bid for Democratic presidential nomination

*1984* Shirley Chisholm founds National Political Caucus of Black Women

*1984* Wynton Marsalis wins Grammy Awards for jazz and classical music

*1984* *The Cosby Show* premiers on NBC, eventually becoming top-rated series on television

*1984* Carl Lewis wins four Gold Medals at Olympics in Los Angeles, matching record set by Jesse Owens in 1936

*1984* Walter Payton becomes leading rusher in pro football history

*1984* Russell Simmons founds Def Jam Records

*1985* African-American artists lead collaboration that produces "We Are the World" single to raise funds for famine relief in Africa

*1985* Gwendolyn Brooks named US Poet Laureate:

*1984* Bishop Desmond Mpilo Tutu of South Africa wins Nobel Peace Prize

*1984–85* More than a million die in Ethiopian famine

*1985* Live Aid concert held in London, Philadelphia, Sydney, and Moscow, for Ethiopian famine relief

## "Poetry is life distilled."

*1985* Grambling State University's Eddie Robinson becomes winningest coach in college football history

*1985* Inspired by humanitarian Harry Belafonte, "We Are the World" written by Michael Jackson and Lionel Ritchie and conducted and produced by Quincy Jones to raise money and provide food relief to Ethiopia

*1985* South African president P. W. Botha offers release to Mandela, provided he will "reject violence as a political instrument"; Mandela refuses

*1986* Americans celebrate first annual Martin Luther King Jr. federal holiday

*1986* Wole Soyinka of Nigeria first black African to win Nobel Prize in Literature

*1986* Black astronaut Ronald McNair among crew members who die on space shuttle *Challenger*

*1986* Oprah Winfrey first African-American woman to host nationally syndicated television show

*1986* Spike Lee emerges as major new filmmaker with *She's Gotta Have It*

*1986* Mike Tyson, at 20, becomes youngest heavyweight champion in history

*1987* August Wilson's *Fences* wins Pulitzer Prize and Tony Award

*1987* Guyanese historian Ivan Van Sertima publishes controversial book *They Came Before Columbus: The African Presence in Ancient America*

*1987* Rita Dove wins Pulitzer Prize for Poetry

*1987* The film *Yeleen* (*Light*), by Souleymane Cissé of Mali, wins Jury Prize at Cannes Film Festival

*1987* Johnnetta B. Cole becomes first African-American woman president of Spelman College in Atlanta

*1987* "Queen of Soul" Aretha Franklin first woman inducted into Rock and Roll Hall of Fame

*1987* Reginald Lewis first African-American CEO of billion-dollar corporation with acquisition of Beatrice Foods:

**"I've never liked hearing people say you can't do this or you can't do that."**

*1987* Brigadier Gen. Fred A. Gordon becomes first Commandant of Cadets, US Military Academy at West Point

*1987* Studio Museum in Harlem organizes major exhibition of Harlem Renaissance art

*1987* Sammy Davis Jr. honored at Kennedy Center

*1988* Jesse Jackson receives 1,218 delegate votes at Democratic National Convention but loses presidential nomination to Michael Dukakis

*1988* Bill Cosby's gift of $20 million to Spelman College largest ever made by black American to college or university

*1988* More than 60,000 marchers return to site of 1963 March on Washington to commemorate 25th anniversary

*1988* Carl Lewis, Florence Griffith-Joyner, and Jackie Joyner-Kersee dominate track and field events at Seoul Olympics

*1989* Rev. Barbara Harris elected first woman bishop of Episcopal Church

*1989* Ronald H. Brown becomes first African-American chair of Democratic National Committee

*1989* Frederick Drew Gregory becomes first African American to command space shuttle

*1989* Gen. Colin Powell first African-American chair of US Joint Chiefs of Staff

*1989* L. Douglas Wilder of Virginia elected first African-American governor of a state on same day that David Dinkins becomes first black mayor of New York City

*1988* Nordic countries implement comprehensive sanctions against South Africa and South West Africa (present-day Namibia) to counteract apartheid

*1988* Pope John Paul II makes apostolic voyage to Zimbabwe, Botswana, Lesotho, Swaziland and Mozambique

*1988* South Africa agrees to remove its 50,000 troops from Namibia, in exchange for Cuba's withdrawal of its 50,000 from Angola

*1988* At ninth summit of Caribbean Community and Common Market (CARICOM), leaders of 13 Caribbean nations agree to remove nearly all barriers to trade within region

*1989* South African government starts dismantling six nuclear fission devices

*1989* World Health Organization African Regional Office adopts global goal of eradicating polio by 2000

*1989* Film *Yaaba (Grandmother)*, by Idrissa Ouédraogo of Burkina Faso, wins international critics' prize at Cannes

*1989* Bill White becomes first African-American league president when chosen to head baseball's National League

*1989* Art Shell becomes first African-American head coach in National Football League history when hired by Oakland Raiders

*1989* Denzel Washington wins the Academy Award for Best Supporting Actor in *Glory*

*1989* Martinique-born Euzhan Palcy directs antiapartheid film *A Dry White Season*, becoming first woman of African descent to direct Hollywood studio movie

*1989* Dallas Museum of Art organizes and tours "Black Art: Ancestral Legacy" exhibition

*1990* African-American population reaches 29,986,060 (12 percent)

*1990* August Wilson wins Pulitzer Prize for play *The Piano Lesson*

*1990* Recently freed South African leader Nelson Mandela welcomed to New York City by Mayor Dinkins after 27 years' incarceration

*1990* Sharon Pratt Kelly first black woman to be elected mayor of Washington, DC

*1990* Charles Johnson wins National Book Award for his novel *Middle Passage*

*1990* Quincy Jones earns record 76th Grammy Award nomination

*1991* Clarence Thomas nominated to replace retired US Supreme Court Justice Thurgood Marshall

*1990* Nelson Mandela released from prison after serving nearly 28 years; Mandela and the ANC agree to suspension of armed struggle

*1991* At first ANC conference held in South Africa, Nelson Mandela elected president, and Oliver Tambo named ANC Chairman

*1991* African Americans nearly 25 percent of troops engaged in Operation Desert Storm, US war in Iraq

*1991* Physicist Walter Massey becomes first African-American director of National Science Foundation

*1991* Videotape of savage beating of Rodney King by Los Angeles police triggers nationwide outrage

*1992* Derek Walcott, Boston University instructor born in St. Lucia, becomes first black writer from Americas to win Nobel Prize for Literature

*1992* Acquittal of Los Angeles policemen involved in Rodney King beating leads to riots, costing 58 lives and millions of dollars in property damage

*1992* Carol Moseley Braun of Illinois becomes first African-American woman elected to US Senate

*1992* President Bill Clinton names four African Americans to cabinet posts

*1992* Mae Carol Jemison first African-American woman in space

*1992* Spike Lee releases epic film, *Malcolm X*

*1993* Toni Morrison becomes first African-American woman to win Nobel Prize for Literature:

*1991* Afro-French skater Surya Bonaly wins first of five European Figure Skating Championships

*1992* Civil war and famine in Somalia attract worldwide attention

*1992* US Marines land near Mogadishu, Somalia, ahead of a UN peacekeeping force; withdraw in 1994 after "Black Hawk Down" incident

*1993* Nobel Peace Prize awarded to Nelson Mandela and F. W. de Klerk

"We die. That may be the meaning of life. But we do language. That may be the measure of our lives."
—MORRISON'S NOBEL LECTURE

*1993* Maya Angelou reads specially commissioned poem, "On the Pulse of Morning," at the inauguration of President Bill Clinton

*1993* Rita Dove named US Poet Laureate

*1993* M. Joycelyn Elders first African American and second woman named Surgeon General of US

*1993* African-American playwright George C. Wolfe becomes head of Public Theater in New York City

*1993* Michael Jordan leads Chicago Bulls to third straight NBA title

*1994* African Americans hold 38 seats in Congress but lose three committee chairs in Republican takeover

*1994* Len Coleman becomes president of baseball's National League

*1994* Marion Barry elected to fourth term as mayor of Washington, DC

*1994* Nelson Mandela becomes first democratically elected president of South Africa

*1994* Violence in Rwanda kills some 800,000 people, about 10 percent of population

*1995* More than one million African-American men respond to Louis Farrakhan's call for Million Man March in Washington, DC

*1995* Shirley Jackson heads US Nuclear Regulatory Commission

*1995* O. J. Simpson acquitted of murder of ex-wife and her friend, with Johnnie Cochran as lead attorney

*1995* Dr. Helene Gayle becomes first woman and first African-American director of National Center for HIV, SID STD, and TB Prevention in US Centers for Disease Control

*1995* Nigerian author Ken Saro-Wiwa, leader of Movement for the Survival of the Ogoni People, and eight others in movement, executed by Nigerian military following nonviolent protests against Shell Oil

*1996* First African American Commerce Secretary Ron Brown killed in plane crash near Dubrovnik, Croatia

*1996* California voters pass Proposition 209, outlawing affirmative action policies throughout state

*1996* Texaco settles largest discrimination suit in US history, awarding $176 million to 1,400 current and former African-American employees

*1996* Ghanaian diplomat Kofi Annan named Secretary General of the United Nations

*1996* Ethiopian Fatuma Roba first African woman to become Olympic marathon champion

*1996* Sprinter Michael Johnson first man to win both 200-meter and 400-meter Olympic events

*1996 Bring in 'Da Noise, Bring in 'Da Funk,* history of tap dance by George Wolfe and Savion Glover, wins four Tony Awards

*1996* Classical composer George Walker first African American to win Pulitzer Prize for Music

*1997* Wynton Marsalis's *Blood on the Fields* first jazz composition to win Pulitzer Prize for Music

*1997* Zaire president Mobutu Sese Seko deposed, flees country, and dies in exile in Morocco

*1997* Corcoran Gallery of Art in Washington, DC, mounts career retrospective on Gordon Parks, groundbreaking African-American photographer, film director, and journalist

*1997* Princess Diana walks through minefield in Angola and calls for international ban on landmines

*1997* Contemporary artist Kara Walker, at 28 one of youngest people to receive MacArthur Fellowship

*1997 Volume III: The Slave Societies of the Caribbean* of UNESCO's *General History of the Caribbean* is first of six volumes to be published

*1997* Tiger Woods first African American to win Masters Golf Tournament in Augusta, Georgia

*1997* Congressional Medals of Honor awarded belatedly to seven African Americans for heroism in World War II

*1997* Jesse Jackson launches Wall Street Project:

**"So we have gone from sharecroppers to shareholders. We say to corporate America: We don't want to be just consumers and workers, but investors and partners."**

*1997* Hundreds of thousands of African-American women gather in Philadelphia, Pennsylvania, for Million Woman March

*1997* President Clinton makes formal apology to black men exploited in US Public Health Service Tuskegee Syphilis Study

*1997* Eddie Robinson retires as Louisiana's Grambling State University football coach after 57 seasons and record 408 victories

*1998* John Hope Franklin heads President's Commission on Race to promote national dialog on issues affecting blacks in US, and at PUSH rally in Chicago admonishes critics who claim commission has no members with opposing views:

*1998* Nigerian journalist Christina Anyanwu wins UNESCO/Guillermo Cano World Press Freedom Prize

*1998* In Rwanda, former prime minister Jean Kambanda sentenced to life imprisonment for his part in 1994 genocide

**"I didn't know there was an opposing view to justice."**

*1998* Julian Bond becomes chair of National NAACP Board of Directors

*1998* The *Pittsburgh Courier* wins Polk Award for role as top print news source of interest to black Americans

*1998* Michael Jordan leads Chicago Bulls to sixth NBA title in eight years

*1998* Three white supremacists in Jasper, Texas, chain James Byrd Jr. to back of pickup truck, drag him to his death, and dismember his body

*1999* Serena Williams wins US Open Women's Singles tennis championship

*1999* Mpule Kwelagobe of Botswana wins Miss Universe beauty pageant, becoming first black African-born woman to hold title

*1999* *Time* magazine votes Jamaican reggae artist Bob Marley & the Wailers' *Exodus* "Album of the Century"

*1999* In South Africa's second democratic election, former deputy president Thabo Mbeki succeeds Nelson Mandela

*1999* Chief Olusegun Obasanjo elected president of Nigeria

*2000* African-American population 34,658,190 (12.3 percent)

*2000* Venus Williams wins tennis singles titles at both Wimbledon and US Open

*2000* Tulsa, Oklahoma, Riot Commission recommends to Oklahoma state legislature that reparations be paid to survivors of 1921 Tulsa race riots

*2000* General Colin Powell and Stanford University Provost Condoleezza Rice named Secretary of State and National Security Advisor respectively by President-elect George W. Bush

*2001* September 11 attacks by al-Qaeda in New York and Washington, D.C., kill approximately 3,000, destroy World Trade Center, damage Pentagon, and crash plane in Pennsylvania

*2001* Thomas Blanton Jr. sentenced to life in prison for his role in 1963 deaths of four girls during the bombing of 16th Street Baptist Church in Birmingham, Alabama

*2001* Hispanics become nation's largest minority group in US, replacing African Americans

*2001* David Levering Lewis wins second Pulitzer Prize for Biography for *W. E. B. Du Bois: The Fight for Equality and the American Century, 1919–1963*; he won first Pulitzer Prize for first volume of this landmark work on the life of Du Bois

*2001* Dennis Haysbert begins his ongoing role as black US president on hit TV show *24*

*2000* In Ghana, John Kufuor elected president after former coup leader Jerry Rawlings's 19-year domination of Ghanaian politics

*2001* World Conference Against Racism held in Durban, South Africa

*2001* Secretary of State Colin Powell instructs US representatives to leave World Conference on Racism in Durban, South Africa, saying notion that "Zionism equals racism" is wrong

*2001* Nigeria, South Africa, and Algeria launch New Partnership for African Development (NE), an economic development program

*2001* Secretary-General Kofi Annan and United Nations receive Nobel Peace Prize

**2002** FleetBoston Financial and Aetna insurance companies among corporations named in federal lawsuit seeking billions of dollars in reparations for descendants of enslaved Africans from corporations that benefited from slavery

**2002** Bobby Frank Cherry found guilty of first-degree murder for his role in the 1963 16th Street Baptist Church bombings

**2002** Suzan-Lori Parks wins Pulitzer Prize for Drama for *Top Dog/Under Dog*

**2002** Denzel Washington, Halle Berry, and Will Smith nominated for Academy Awards; Berry becomes first black woman to win in Best Actress category, while Washington wins Best Actor award

**2002** Activist, poet, and playwright Amiri Baraka, named Poet Laureate of New Jersey, asked to resign after reading poem implying that New York Israelis were forewarned about 9/11 attacks on World Trade Center

**2003** Marc Morial, former Mayor of New Orleans, named head of National Urban League succeeding Hugh Price

**2003** Supreme Court, in two split decisions, strikes down University of Michigan race-based affirmative action program while affirming structured programs that encourage minority law school applicants

**2003** William H. Gray III, former US congressman, announces his retirement as president of United Negro College Fund

**2003** Activist Rev. Al Sharpton launches his campaign for US presidency

**2003** Michael Jordan retires as basketball player for third and final time

**2002** At 53-nation summit of African leaders in Durban, South Africa, Organization of African Unity (OAU) and African Economic Community (AEC) combine to form African Union

**2002** World Health Organization struggles to contain breakout of Ebola in Republic of the Congo, on border near Gabon

**2002** Violence mars national election in Zimbabwe; President Robert Mugabe pledges "fair and free" elections in next balloting

**2003** AIDS Conference in Durban; an estimated 4.5 million South Africans infected with HIV—highest number in any country in the world

**2003** First conference of African-descended legislators from the Americas and the Caribbean held in Brasilia, Brazil

**2003** Conflict in Darfur between government and warring factions leaves tens of thousands without homes

**2004** Sean "P. Diddy" Combs makes his Broadway acting debut in revival of Lorraine Hansberry's *A Raisin in the Sun*

**2004** Phylicia Rashad becomes first African-American woman to win best actress Tony Award for her role in *A Raisin in the Sun*

**2004** Douglas Wilder, former governor of Virginia, is elected mayor of Richmond, Virginia

**2004** Chair of US Civil Rights Commission, Mary Frances Berry, resigns

**2004** August Wilson's *Gem of the Ocean* opens on Broadway in December, completing his ten-play cycle on the black experience in America; Wilson dies of cancer following October

**2005** Condoleezza Rice, former US National Security Advisor, named Secretary of State, first black woman to hold the office

**2005** *Essence*, nation's most popular black women's magazine, sells majority of its ownership to Time, Inc.

**2005** Actors Jamie Foxx and Morgan Freeman awarded best actor and best supporting actor Oscars at 77th annual Academy Awards

**2005** Hurricanes Katrina and Rita destroy parts of Louisiana, Alabama, and Mississippi, killing over 1,000 and displacing thousands more; New Orleans hardest hit and its black, low-income residents suffer some of greatest losses; Bush Administration fails to respond in timely and effective manner

**2004** Jean Bertrand Aristide, Haiti's first democratically elected president, resigns, flees Haiti in midst of national chaos, saying he was "kidnapped" by US and taken by force to Central African Republic

**2004** Kenyan ecologist Wangari Maathai is first African woman to win Nobel Peace Prize

**2005** Main Hutu rebel group (FDLR) apologizes for Rwandan genocide, offers to disarm

**2005** Ellen Johnson-Sirleaf becomes first African woman to head an African nation when elected president of Liberia

*2005* Edgar Ray Killen, an 80-year-old former Klansman, convicted of 1964 murders of three Civil Rights workers in Mississippi

*2005* Rev. Jesse L. Jackson leads effort to urge Congress to renew Voting Rights Act, which was set to expire in 2007

*2005* Verizon executive Bruce S. Gordon named new president of the NAACP

*2005* Nation of Islam commemorates the 10th anniversary of the Million Man March, with a Millions More Movement gathering in Washington, DC

*2006* Tavis Smiley's *The Covenant with Black America,* published by African-American–owned Third World Press, becomes *New York Times* bestseller

*2006* *Guinness Book of World Records* names pop singer Whitney Houston "most awarded female artist of all time"

*2006* Actress LaChanze wins Tony Award for best lead actress in musical for her role in *The Color Purple* on Broadway

*2006* New York City's African Burial Ground in lower Manhattan designated a National Monument within National Parks system, putting it on a par with the Statute of Liberty and other National Monuments

*2006* Former Harlem State Senator David Paterson elected Lieutenant Governor of the State of New York

*2006* Ground broken for national memorial to Rev. Martin Luther King Jr. on National Mall in Washington, DC

*2006* US Secretary of State Condoleezza Rice presses Sudan's government to accept United Nations force in war-torn region of Darfur

*2006* Anglican Church (Church of England) formally apologizes to people of African descent for Britain's role in transatlantic slave trade

*2006* Portia Simpson-Miller, elected president of governing People's National Party of Jamaica, becomes nation's first female prime minister

*2006* Seven thousand African Union (AU) troops deployed in Darfur, but fail to end conflict that left millions of people in overcrowded camps and over 100,000 dead

*2006* Cuban premier Fidel Castro, during long illness, transfers power to his younger brother, Raúl Castro; announcement sparks major celebrations in Miami, Florida, among exiled Cubans

*2006* Ghanaian Kofi Annan, Secretary General of the United Nations, completes his second five-year term of office

*2007* Congressman Charles B. Rangel becomes first African-American chairman of House Ways and Means Committee

*2007* First ever meeting of teams coached by black NFL head coaches occurs when Lovie Smith of the Chicago Bears and Tony Dungy of the Indianapolis Colts square off in Super Bowl XLI; Dungy becomes first black NFL head coach to win Super Bowl

*2007* Forest Whitaker wins best actor Academy Award for his role as Idi Amin in *The Last King of Scotland*

*2007* Jennifer Hudson wins the best supporting actress Oscar for her role in *Dreamgirls*

*2007* Choreographer Bill T. Jones wins Tony Award for Best Choreography for *Spring Awakening*

*2007* Venus Williams wins Women's Singles championship in tennis at Wimbledon for fourth time

*2007* Harsh sentencing of six black teens accused of beating white schoolmate in Jena, Louisiana, sparks national protest and march of over 30,000 in Jena in support of the teenagers

*2007* Barry Bonds surpasses Hank Aaron's Major League baseball home run record amid charges he used performance enhancing drugs to achieve this goal

*2007* African Burial Ground National Monument memorial dedicated in three-day tribute program

*2007* Black CEOs Richard Parsons of Time Warner, Inc., and Stanley O'Neal of Merrill Lynch resign

*2007* Oprah Winfrey opens leadership academy for girls in South Africa

*2007* Security Council authorizes deployment of hybrid UN and African Union force to Darfur

*2007* US carries out air strikes in southern Somalia, targeting suspected Al-Qaeda training camps

*2007* UN Security Council authorizes six-month African Union peacekeeping mission for Somalia

**2007** David Paterson becomes first black governor of New York after Eliot Spitzer forced to resign

**2008** Senator Barack Obama of Illinois becomes Democratic Party's first African-American nominee for US presidency

**2008** US House of Representatives issues a formal apology to black Americans for the "fundamental injustice, cruelty, brutality and inhumanity of slavery and Jim Crow" segregation

**2008** Barack Obama wins over Senator John McCain of Arizona to become 44th US president, and first African-American president

**2008** The United Nations estimates that conflict in Darfur has left as many as 400,000 dead from violence and disease

**2008** In Zimbabwe elections, President Robert Mugabe's ruling party loses control of Parliament; he eventually agrees to a power-sharing deal negotiated by South African President Thabo Mbeki that names opposition leader Morgan Tsvangirai as Prime Minister

**2008** South African President Thabo Mbeki resigns after a bitter power struggle with Jacob Zuma, head of the African National Congress (ANC), and is replaced by Zuma's deputy Kgalema Motlanthe, who is eligible as a member of Parliament

**2008** In Beijing, Jamaican sprinter Usain "Lightning" Bolt first man in history to set world records in 100 meters, 200 meters, and 4 × 100 meters

# PART TWO

## Key Texts, Literary Works & Records

# Charters, Petitions & Acts

## THE DECLARATION OF INDEPENDENCE

*July 4, 1776*

Although the Declaration of Independence that he drafted immediately became the world's leading manifesto celebrating human rights and personal freedom, Thomas Jefferson owned over two hundred slaves when he wrote it. African Americans used similar language to make their freedom claims.

*Excerpt:*

The unanimous Declaration of the thirteen united States of America,

When in the Course of human events, it becomes necessary for one people to dissolve the political bands which have connected them with another, and to assume among the powers of the earth, the separate and equal station to which the Laws of Nature and of Nature's God entitle them, a decent respect to the opinions of mankind requires that they should declare the causes which impel them to the separation.

We hold these truths to be self-evident, that all men are created equal, that they are endowed by their Creator with certain unalienable Rights, that among these are Life, Liberty and the pursuit of Happiness.—That to secure these rights, Governments are instituted among Men, deriving their just powers from the consent of the governed,—That whenever any Form of Government becomes destructive of these ends, it is the Right of the People to alter or to abolish it, and to institute new Government, laying its foundation on such principles and organizing its powers in such form, as to them shall seem most likely to effect their Safety and Happiness.

# STATEMENT FROM MEETING OF
# NEW YORK NEGROES

*January 25, 1831, New York*

A black mass meeting was held in 1831 to protest the recently organized
American Colonization Society's initiative to send free blacks to Africa.

*Excerpt:*

We do not believe that things will always continue the same. The time must
come when the Declaration of Independence will be felt in the heart as well
as uttered from the mouth, and when the rights of all shall be properly
acknowledged and appreciated. God hasten that time. This is our home, and
this is our country. Beneath its sod lie the bones of our fathers; for it, some
of them fought, bled and died. Here we were born, and here we will die.

# THE EMANCIPATION PROCLAMATION

*Abraham Lincoln* — *January 1, 1863*

Issued on the eve of the third year of the nation's civil war, the proclamation ostensibly freed enslaved Africans in the rebellious states but did not
abolish slavery in states loyal to the Union. More significantly, it authorized
the use of black men in the Union Army and Navy. Almost two hundred
thousand blacks eventually fought for the Union and black freedom.

Whereas, on the twenty-second day of September, in the year of our Lord
one thousand eight hundred and sixty-two, a proclamation was issued by
the President of the United States, containing, among other things, the
following, to wit:

"That on the first day of January, in the year of our Lord one thousand
eight hundred and sixty-three, all persons held as slaves within any State or
designated part of a State, the people whereof shall then be in rebellion
against the United States, shall be then, thenceforward, and forever free;
and the Executive Government of the United States, including the military
and naval authority thereof, will recognize and maintain the freedom of
such persons, and will do no act or acts to repress such persons, or any of
them, in any efforts they may make for their actual freedom.

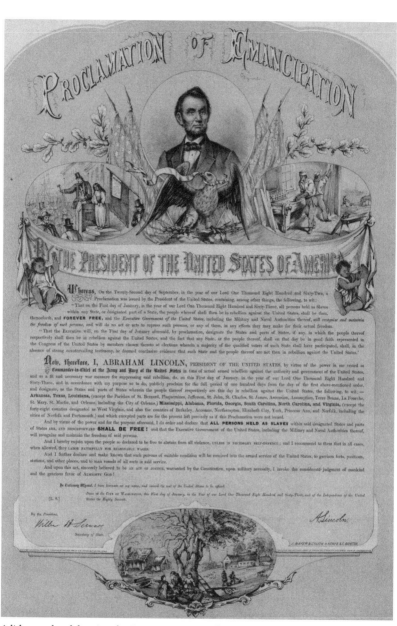

A lithograph celebrating the Emancipation Proclamation, c. 1863

"That the Executive will, on the first day of January aforesaid, by proclamation, designate the States and parts of States, if any, in which the people thereof, respectively, shall then be in rebellion against the United States; and the fact that any State, or the people thereof, shall on that day be, in good faith, represented in the Congress of the United States by members chosen thereto at elections wherein a majority of the qualified voters of such State shall have participated, shall, in the absence of strong countervailing testimony, be deemed conclusive evidence that such State, and the people thereof, are not then in rebellion against the United States."

Now, therefore I, Abraham Lincoln, President of the United States, by virtue of the power in me vested as Commander-in-Chief, of the Army and Navy of the United States in time of actual armed rebellion against the authority and government of the United States, and as a fit and necessary war measure for suppressing said rebellion, do, on this first day of January, in the year of our Lord one thousand eight hundred and sixty-three, and in accordance with my purpose so to do publicly proclaimed for the full period of one hundred days, from the day first above mentioned, order and designate as the States and parts of States wherein the people thereof respectively, are this day in rebellion against the United States, the following, to wit:

Arkansas, Texas, Louisiana, (except the Parishes of St. Bernard, Plaquemines, Jefferson, St. John, St. Charles, St. James Ascension, Assumption, Terrebonne, Lafourche, St. Mary, St. Martin, and Orleans, including the City of New Orleans) Mississippi, Alabama, Florida, Georgia, South Carolina, North Carolina, and Virginia, (except the forty-eight counties designated as West Virginia, and also the counties of Berkley, Accomac, Northampton, Elizabeth City, York, Princess Ann, and Norfolk, including the cities of Norfolk and Portsmouth[)], and which excepted parts, are for the present, left precisely as if this proclamation were not issued.

And by virtue of the power, and for the purpose aforesaid, I do order and declare that all persons held as slaves within said designated States, and parts of States, are, and henceforward shall be free; and that the Executive government of the United States, including the military and naval authorities thereof, will recognize and maintain the freedom of said persons.

And I hereby enjoin upon the people so declared to be free to abstain from all violence, unless in necessary self-defence; and I recommend to them that, in all cases when allowed, they labor faithfully for reasonable wages.

And I further declare and make known, that such persons of suitable condition, will be received into the armed service of the United States to garrison forts, positions, stations, and other places, and to man vessels of all sorts in said service.

And upon this act, sincerely believed to be an act of justice, warranted by the Constitution, upon military necessity, I invoke the considerate judgment of mankind, and the gracious favor of Almighty God.

In witness whereof, I have hereunto set my hand and caused the seal of the United States to be affixed.

Done at the City of Washington, this first day of January, in the year of our Lord one thousand eight hundred and sixty three, and of the Independence of the United States of America the eighty-seventh.

# PETITION TO CONGRESS OF NATIONAL EQUAL RIGHTS LEAGUE

*Cleveland, Ohio, 1865*

The National Equal Rights League grew out of the Syracuse National Negro Convention of 1864 to advocate for the rights of black people through appeals to conscience and via legal processes. The petition from the Cleveland meeting in 1865 called for a constitutional amendment barring all Jim Crow legislation.

The undersigned, officers and members of the National Equal Rights League call the attention of your honorable body to the 4th Article of the United States Constitution, Section 4th, in which we find that "the United States shall guarantee to every State in the Union a Republican form of government"; and seeing that in many States such a form of government does not exist, we therefore most respectfully ask the adoption of the following amendment to the Constitution of the United States:

That there shall be no legislation within the limits of the United States and Territories, against any civilized portion of the inhabitants, native-born or naturalized, on account of race or color, and that all such legislation now existing within said limits is anti-republican in character, and therefore void.

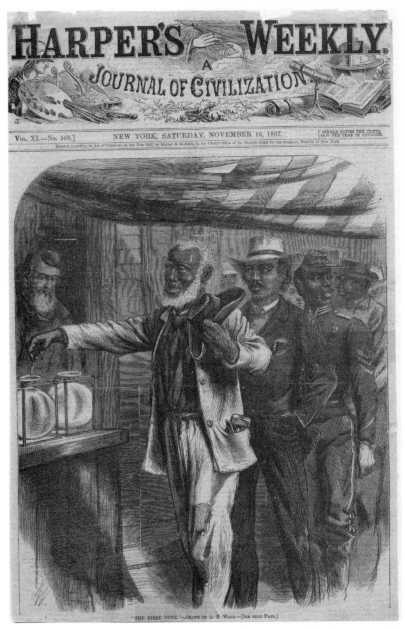

HARPER'S WEEKLY.

A JOURNAL OF CIVILIZATION.

VOL. XI.—No. 568.]　　　NEW YORK, SATURDAY, NOVEMBER 16, 1867.　　　[ SINGLE COPIES TEN CENTS.
$4.00 PER YEAR IN ADVANCE.

Entered according to Act of Congress, in the Year 1867, by Harper & Brothers, in the Clerk's Office of the District Court for the Southern District of New York.

"THE FIRST VOTE."—DRAWN BY A. R. WAUD.—[SEE NEXT PAGE.]

A *Harper's Weekly* cover from November 16, 1867 shows Virginian freedmen voting for the first time.

# AMENDMENTS TO THE CONSTITUTION OF THE UNITED STATES

*1865–70*

Three Reconstruction amendments ratified between 1865 and 1870 opened the door to full citizenship for African Americans: the 13th abolishing slavery, the 14th guaranteeing citizenship, and the 15th giving black men the right to vote. The promise of the 15th Amendment was not fully realized until almost a century after its ratification in 1870. Southern states employed poll taxes, literacy tests, and other measures to effectively disenfranchise African Americans. The majority of African Americans in the South were not registered to vote until the passage of the Voting Rights Act of 1965.

## Excerpt of 13th Amendment to the US Constitution:
### Abolition of Slavery ⟶ *Ratified 1865*

Section 1. Neither slavery nor involuntary servitude, except as a punishment for crime whereof the party shall have been duly convicted, shall exist within the United States, or any place subject to their jurisdiction.

## Excerpt of 14th Amendment to the US Constitution:
### Civil Rights ⟶ *Ratified 1868*

Section 1. All persons born or naturalized in the United States, and subject to the jurisdiction thereof, are citizens of the United States and of the State wherein they reside. No State shall make or enforce any law which shall abridge the privileges or immunities of citizens of the United States; nor shall any State deprive any person of life, liberty, or property, without due process of law; nor deny to any person within its jurisdiction the equal protection of the laws.

## Excerpt of 15th Amendment to the US Constitution:
### Voting Rights ⟶ *Ratified 1870*

Section 1. The right of citizens of the United States to vote shall not be denied or abridged by the United States or by any State on account of race, color, or previous condition of servitude.

# FOUNDING CONVENTION OF THE AFRO-AMERICAN LEAGUE

*Chicago, Illinois, 1890*

A group of 147 delegates from 21 states and the District of Columbia met to form this national organization to advocate for equal rights and to organize and encourage state and local affiliates in efforts to break down color barriers. The delegates adopted this sarcastic response to a series of congressional legislative proposals to fund black deportation from the South.

*A Petition to Congress:*

Whereas, The predominance of Afro-Americans in the States of Alabama, South Carolina, Louisiana, Mississippi, and other Southern States makes the situation painful and uncomfortable for the small minority of white fellow citizens residing therein; therefore, be it

*Resolved*, That we do petition the Honorable Congress of the United States to make and provide for an appropriation of $10,000,000,000 to furnish the unhappy white citizens of these States, who may desire to settle in other and more favored States, free from Afro-American majorities, with free transportation and lunch by the way to any of the States north of the Mason Dixon line. Be it further

*Resolved*, That the Congress designate Senator Morgan, of Alabama; Senator Hampton, of South Carolina, and Senator Gibson, of Tennessee, to be the "Moses" to lead the unhappy people out of the States of their misfortune.

# EXECUTIVE ORDER 8802

*President Franklin D. Roosevelt* ── *June 25, 1941*

A. Philip Randolph issued a call to black Americans for a March on
Washington on July 1, 1941, to demand that President Roosevelt
outlaw racial discrimination in the defense industries and the armed
forces. Under pressure, the President issued this executive order and
Randolph called off the planned demonstration. Black men and
women worked in the defense industries during World War II.

*Excerpt:*

Reaffirming Policy Of Full Participation In The Defense Program By All
Persons, Regardless Of Race, Creed, Color, Or National Origin, And
Directing Certain Action In Furtherance Of Said Policy

WHEREAS it is the policy of the United States to encourage full participation in the national defense program by all citizens of the United States,
regardless of race, creed, color, or national origin, in the firm belief that
the democratic way of life within the Nation can be defended successfully
only with the help and support of all groups within its borders; and

WHEREAS there is evidence that available and needed workers have been
barred from employment in industries engaged in defense production
solely because of considerations of race, creed, color, or national origin, to
the detriment of workers' morale and of national unity:

NOW, THEREFORE, by virtue of the authority vested in me by the
Constitution and the statutes, and as a prerequisite to the successful
conduct of our national defense production effort, I do hereby reaffirm
the policy of the United States that there shall be no discrimination in the
employment of workers in defense industries or government because of
race, creed, color, or national origin, and I do hereby declare that it is the
duty of employers and of labor organizations, in furtherance of said
policy and of this order, to provide for the full and equitable participation
of all workers in defense industries, without discrimination because of
race, creed, color, or national origin; . . .

# THE CIVIL RIGHTS ACT OF 1964

*July 2, 1964*

As the nation watched the often brutal response to the nonviolent civil rights protests of the late 1950s into the 1960s, President John F. Kennedy was prompted to send a bill to Congress that would become the Civil Rights Act of 1964. It was signed into law by President Lyndon Johnson.

*Excerpt:*

An Act. To enforce the constitutional right to vote, to confer jurisdiction upon the district courts of the United States to provide injunctive relief against discrimination in public accommodations, to authorize the Attorney General to institute suits to protect constitutional rights in public facilities and public education, to extend the Commission on Civil Rights, to prevent discrimination in federally assisted programs, to establish a Commission on Equal Employment Opportunity, and for other purposes.

Be it enacted by the Senate and House of Representatives of the United States of America in Congress assembled, That this Act may be cited as the "Civil Rights Act of 1964."

# THE VOTING RIGHTS ACT OF 1965

*August 6, 1965*

By the summer of 1964, voting rights had become a dominant issue in the civil rights movement in the South. Following the murder of voting rights activists in Philadelphia, Mississippi, that summer and the "Bloody Sunday" attack by law enforcement officers on civil rights marchers on the Edmund Pettus Bridge in Selma, Alabama, in March 1965, President Lyndon Johnson addressed Congress on March 15 to present his voting rights bill, ending with the words of the civil rights anthem, "We shall overcome." He signed the Voting Rights Act five months later.

*Excerpt:*

AN ACT To enforce the fifteenth amendment to the Constitution of the United States, and for other purposes.

Be it enacted by the Senate and House of Representatives of the United States of America in Congress assembled, That this Act shall be known as the "Voting Rights Act of 1965."

SEC. 2. No voting qualification or prerequisite to voting, or standard, practice, or procedure shall be imposed or applied by any State or political subdivision to deny or abridge the right of any citizen of the United States to vote on account of race or color.

President Lyndon Johnson signs the voting rights bill.

# Speeches

## AN ADDRESS TO THE NEW ENGLAND
## ANTI-SLAVERY SOCIETY

*Maria Stewart* — *New England Anti-Slavery Society, Boston, September 21, 1832*

Maria Stewart, who had gained public recognition as a contributor
to the antislavery newspaper the *Liberator*, was the first woman of
any race to deliver an address to a mixed-gender audience on
political issues.

*Excerpt:*

Few white persons of either sex, who are calculated for any thing else, are
willing to spend their lives and bury their talents in performing mean, servile
labor. And such is the horrible idea that I entertain respecting a life of servitude, that if I conceived of there being no possibility of my rising above the
condition of a servant, I would gladly hail death as a welcome messenger. O,
horrible idea, indeed! to possess noble souls aspiring after high and honorable
acquirements, yet confined by the chains of ignorance and poverty to lives of
continual drudgery and toil. Neither do I know of any who have enriched
themselves by spending their lives as house-domestics, washing windows,
shaking carpets, brushing boots, or tending upon gentlemen's tables. I can
but die for expressing my sentiments; and I am as willing to die by the sword
as the pestilence; for I am a true born American; your blood flows in my
veins, and your spirit fires my breast.

I observed a piece in the *Liberator* a few months since, stating that the colo-
nizationists had published a work respecting us, asserting that we were
lazy and idle. I confute them on that point. Take us generally as a people,
we are neither lazy nor idle; and considering how little we have to excite
or stimulate us, I am almost astonished that there are so many industrious
and ambitious ones to be found; although I acknowledge, with extreme
sorrow, that there are some who never were and never will be serviceable
to society. And have you not a similar class among yourselves?

Again. It was asserted that we were "a ragged set, crying for liberty." I
reply to it, the whites have so long and so loudly proclaimed the theme of

equal rights and privileges, that our souls have caught the flame also, ragged as we are. As far as our merit deserves, we feel a common desire to rise above the condition of servants and drudges. I have learnt, by bitter experience, that continual hard labor deadens the energies of the soul, and benumbs the faculties of the mind; the ideas become confined, the mind barren, and, like the scorching sands of Arabia, produces nothing; or, like the uncultivated soil, brings forth thorns and thistles.

# THE MEANING OF JULY FOURTH
# FOR THE NEGRO

*Frederick Douglass* — *Rochester, New York, July 4, 1852*

When he was invited by the Rochester Ladies Antislavery Society to deliver the annual Independence Day speech in 1852, Frederick Douglass addressed the issue of American slavery. In the tradition of New York State's black community, he insisted on speaking on July 5. Blacks celebrated emancipation in New York State on July 5, 1827, after being urged by state legislators not to celebrate on the fourth when it took effect, since that day was revered by white citizens as their day of national independence.

*Excerpt:*

Fellow Citizens, I am not wanting in respect for the fathers of this republic. The signers of the Declaration of Independence were brave men. They were great men, too great enough to give frame to a great age. It does not often happen to a nation to raise, at one time, such a number of truly great men. The point from which I am compelled to view them is not, certainly, the most favorable; and yet I cannot contemplate their great deeds with less than admiration. They were statesmen, patriots and heroes, and for the good they did, and the principles they contended for, I will unite with you to honor their memory. . . .

Fellow-citizens, pardon me, allow me to ask, why am I called upon to speak here to-day? What have I, or those I represent, to do with your national independence? Are the great principles of political freedom and of natural justice, embodied in that Declaration of Independence, extended to us? and am I, therefore, called upon to bring our humble offering to the national altar, and to confess the benefits and express devout gratitude for the blessings resulting from your independence to us?

Would to God, both for your sakes and ours, that an affirmative answer could be truthfully returned to these questions! Then would my task be light, and my burden easy and delightful. For who is there so cold, that a nation's sympathy could not warm him? Who so obdurate and dead to the claims of gratitude, that would not thankfully acknowledge such priceless benefits? Who so stolid and selfish, that would not give his voice to swell the hallelujahs of a nation's jubilee, when the chains of servitude had been torn from his limbs? I am not that man. In a case like that, the dumb might eloquently speak, and the "lame man leap as an hart."

But such is not the state of the case. I say it with a sad sense of the disparity between us. I am not included within the pale of glorious anniversary! Your high independence only reveals the immeasurable distance between us. The blessings in which you, this day, rejoice, are not enjoyed in common. The rich inheritance of justice, liberty, prosperity and independence, bequeathed by your fathers, is shared by you, not by me. The sunlight that brought light and healing to you, has brought stripes and death to me. This Fourth [of] July is yours, not mine. You may rejoice, I must mourn. To drag a man in fetters into the grand illuminated temple of liberty, and call upon him to join you in joyous anthems, were inhuman mockery and sacrilegious irony. Do you mean, citizens, to mock me, by asking me to speak to-day? If so, there is a parallel to your conduct. And let me warn you that it is dangerous to copy the example of a nation whose crimes, towering up to heaven, were thrown down by the breath of the Almighty, burying that nation in irrevocable ruin! I can to-day take up the plaintive lament of a peeled and woe-smitten people!

"By the rivers of Babylon, there we sat down. Yea! we wept when we remembered Zion. We hanged our harps upon the willows in the midst thereof. For there, they that carried us away captive, required of us a song; and they who wasted us required of us mirth, saying, Sing us one of the songs of Zion. How can we sing the Lord's song in a strange land? If I forget thee, O Jerusalem, let my right hand forget her cunning. If I do not remember thee, let my tongue cleave to the roof of my mouth."

Fellow-citizens, above your national, tumultuous joy, I hear the mournful wail of millions! whose chains, heavy and grievous yesterday, are, to-day, rendered more intolerable by the jubilee shouts that reach them. If I do forget, if I do not faithfully remember those bleeding children of sorrow this day, "may my right hand forget her cunning, and may my tongue cleave to the roof of my mouth!" To forget them, to pass lightly over their wrongs, and to chime in with the popular theme, would be treason most scandalous and shocking, and would make me a reproach before God and the world. My subject, then, fellow-citizens, is American slavery. I shall see this day and its popular characteristics from the slave's point of view. Standing there identified with the American bondman, making his wrongs mine, I do not hesitate to declare, with all my soul, that the character and conduct of this nation never looked blacker to me than on this 4th of July!

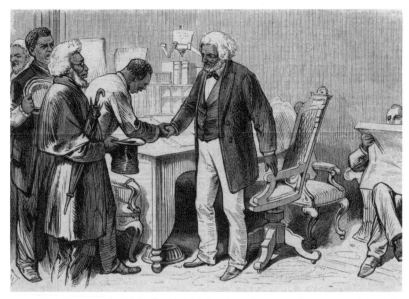

An etching from *Frank Leslie's Illustrated Newspaper* of 1877, with a caption that reads, "Washington, D.C.—The new Administration—Colored Citizens Paying Their Respects to Marshall Frederick Douglass, in his office at the City Hall."

# EXPLANATION OF THE OBJECTS OF THE UNIVERSAL NEGRO IMPROVEMENT ASSOCIATION

*Marcus Garvey* — *Studio recording, New York, July 1921*

This extract from a Universal Negro Improvement Association (UNIA) membership appeal is one of only two known recordings of the voice of Jamaican-born Marcus Garvey, the organization's founder and leader of the back-to-Africa movement. Garvey's vision of a worldwide organization of black people united in their common struggle for freedom and dignity was partially realized in the UNIA, which had chapters throughout the black world.

*Excerpt:*

Fellow citizens of Africa, I greet you in the name of the Universal Negro Improvement Association and African Communities League of the World. You may ask, what organization is that? It is for me to inform you that the Universal Negro Improvement Association is an organization that seeks to unite into one solid body the 400 million Negroes of the world; to link up the 50 million Negroes of the United States of America, with the 20 million Negroes of the West Indies, the 40 million Negroes of South and Central America with the 280 million Negroes of Africa, for the purpose of bettering our industrial, commercial, educational, social and political conditions.

As you are aware, the world in which we live today is divided into separate race groups and different nationalities. Each race and each nationality is endeavoring to work out its own destiny to the exclusion of other races and other nationalities. We hear the cry of England for the Englishman, of France for the Frenchman, of Germany for the Germans, of Ireland for the Irish, of Palestine for the Jews, of Japan for the Japanese, of China for the Chinese.

We of the Universal Negro Improvement Association are raising the cry of Africa for the Africans, those at home and those abroad. There are 400 million Africans in the world who have Negro blood coursing through their veins. And we believe that the time has come to unite these 400 million people for the one common purpose of bettering their condition.

The great problem of the Negro for the last 500 years has been that of disunity. No one or no organization ever took the lead in uniting the Negro race, but within the last four years the Universal Negro Improvement Association has worked wonders in bringing together in one fold four million organized Negroes who are scattered in all parts of the world, being in the 48 states of the American union, all the West Indian Islands, and the countries of South and Central America and Africa. These 40 million people are working to convert the rest of the 400 million scattered all over the world and it is for this purpose that we are asking you to join our ranks and to do the best you can to help us to bring about an emancipated race.

If anything praiseworthy is to be done, it must be done through unity. And it is for that reason that the Universal Negro Improvement Association calls upon every Negro in the United States to rally to its standard. We want to unite the Negro race in this country. We want every Negro to

Marcus Garvey's first UNIA International Convention, 1920, Harlem, New York

work for one common object, that of building a nation of his own on the great continent of Africa. That all Negroes all over the world are working for the establishment of a government in Africa means that it will be realized in another few years.

We want the moral and financial support of every Negro to make the dream a possibility. Already this organization has established itself in Liberia, West Africa, and has endeavored to do all that's possible to develop that Negro country to become a great industrial and commercial commonwealth.

Pioneers have been sent by this organization to Liberia and they are now laying the foundation upon which the 400 million Negroes of the world will build. If you believe that the Negro has a soul, if you believe that the Negro is a man, if you believe the Negro was endowed with the senses commonly given to other men by the Creator, then you must acknowledge that what other men have done, Negroes can do. We want to build up cities, nations, governments, industries of our own in Africa, so that we will be able to have the chance to rise from the lowest to the highest positions in the African commonwealth.

# I HAVE A DREAM

*Martin Luther King Jr.* ⏤ *The March on Washington, August 28, 1963*

The power of the speech delivered by Martin Luther King Jr. at the 1963 March on Washington, which included a coalition of organizations, propelled him into the public consciousness as the leading national civil rights leader.

*Excerpt:*

I am happy to join with you today in what will go down in history as the greatest demonstration for freedom in the history of our nation.

. . . I say to you today, my friends, so even though we face the difficulties of today and tomorrow, I still have a dream. It is a dream deeply rooted in the American dream.

I have a dream that one day this nation will rise up and live out the true meaning of its creed: "We hold these truths to be self-evident: that all men are created equal."

I have a dream that one day on the red hills of Georgia the sons of former slaves and the sons of former slave owners will be able to sit down together at the table of brotherhood.

I have a dream that one day even the state of Mississippi, a state sweltering with the heat of injustice, sweltering with the heat of oppression, will be transformed into an oasis of freedom and justice.

I have a dream that my four little children will one day live in a nation where they will not be judged by the color of their skin but by the content of their character.

I have a dream today.

I have a dream that one day, down in Alabama, with its vicious racists, with its governor having his lips dripping with the words of interposition and nullification; one day right there in Alabama, little black boys and black girls will be able to join hands with little white boys and white girls as sisters and brothers.

I have a dream today.

I have a dream that one day every valley shall be exalted, every hill and mountain shall be made low, the rough places will be made plain, and the crooked places will be made straight, and the glory of the Lord shall be revealed, and all flesh shall see it together.

March on Washington, D.C., August 28, 1963.

# THE BALLOT OR THE BULLET

*Malcolm X* ⟶ *Cory Methodist Church, Cleveland, Ohio, April 3, 1964*

The philosophy articulated by Malcolm X in this speech would become the foundation of the black nationalist movement that emerged in the late 1960s.

*Excerpt:*

No, if you never see me another time in your life, if I die in the morning, I'll die saying one thing: the ballot or the bullet, the ballot or the bullet.

If a Negro in 1964 has to sit around and wait for some cracker senator to filibuster when it comes to the rights of black people, why, you and I should hang our heads in shame. You talk about a march on Washington in 1963, you haven't seen anything. There's some more going down in '64.

And this time they're not going like they went last year. They're not going singing "We Shall Overcome." They're not going with white friends. They're not going with placards already painted for them. They're not going with round-trip tickets. They're going with one-way tickets. And if they don't want that non-nonviolent army going down there, tell them to bring the filibuster to a halt.

The black nationalists aren't going to wait. Lyndon B. Johnson is the head of the Democratic Party. If he's for civil rights, let him go into the Senate next week and declare himself. Let him go in there right now and declare himself. Let him go in there and denounce the Southern branch of his party. Let him go in there right now and take a moral stand—right now, not later. Tell him, don't wait until election time. If he waits too long, brothers and sisters, he will be responsible for letting a condition develop in this country which will create a climate that will bring seeds up out of the ground with vegetation on the end of them looking like something these people never dreamed of. In 1964, it's the ballot or the bullet.

Thank you.

Malcolm X at a rally in New York City, 1963.

Cover of sheet music book, *Songs of the Jubilee Singers from Fisk University*, 1881.

# From Spirituals to Gospel & Pop

## SWING LOW, SWEET CHARIOT

The spirituals "Swing Low, Sweet Chariot" and "Steal Away to Jesus" were songs of praise, but also may have signaled the hope or plan of enslaved Africans to escape to freedom.

*Excerpt:*

*Refrain:*
*Swing low, sweet chariot,*
*Coming for to carry me home*
*Swing low, sweet chariot,*
*Coming for to carry me home*

I looked over Jordan, and what did I see
Coming for to carry me home?
A band of angels coming after me
Coming for to carry me home

*Refrain*

If you get there before I do
Coming for to carry me home
Tell all my friends I coming too
Coming for to carry me home

*Refrain*

I'm sometimes up, I'm sometimes down
Coming for to carry me home
But still my soul feels heavenly bound
Coming for to carry me home . . .

# STEAL AWAY TO JESUS

*Refrain:*
*Steal away, steal away, steal away to Jesus!*
*Steal away, steal away home,*
*I ain't got long to stay here.*

My Lord, He calls me,
He calls me by the thunder;
The trumpet sounds within my soul,
I ain't got long to stay here.

*Refrain*

Green trees are bending,
Poor sinners stand a-trembling;
The trumpet sounds within my soul,
I ain't got long to stay here.

*Refrain*

My Lord, He calls me,
He calls me by the lightning;
The trumpet sounds within my soul,
I ain't got long to stay here.

Fisk Jubilee Singers, c. 1890.

## LIFT EV'RY VOICE AND SING

*James Weldon Johnson* — *1899*

This song was first performed by 500 schoolchildren in segregated
Jacksonville, Florida, to celebrate Abraham Lincoln's birthday on
February 12, 1900. The NAACP later adopted the song as
"The Negro National Anthem."

Lift ev'ry voice and sing,
Till earth and heaven ring,
Ring with the harmonies of Liberty;
Let our rejoicing rise
High as the list'ning skies,
Let it resound loud as the rolling sea.
Sing a song full of the faith that the dark past has taught us,

Sing a song full of the hope that the present has brought us;
Facing the rising sun of our new day begun,
Let us march on till victory is won.

Stony the road we trod,
Bitter the chast'ning rod,
Felt in the days when hope unborn had died;
Yet with a steady beat,
Have not our weary feet
Come to the place for which our fathers sighed?
We have come over a way that with tears has been watered,
We have come, treading our path through the blood of the slaughtered,
Out from the gloomy past,
Till now we stand at last
Where the white gleam of our bright star is cast.

God of our weary years,
God of our silent tears,
Thou who hast brought us thus far on the way;
Thou who hast by Thy might,
Led us into the light,
Keep us forever in the path, we pray.
Lest our feet stray from the places, our God, where we met Thee;
Lest our hearts, drunk with the wine of the world, we forget Thee;
Shadowed beneath Thy hand,
May we forever stand,
True to our God,
True to our native land.

# PRECIOUS LORD, TAKE MY HAND

*Thomas Andrew Dorsey* — *1932*

Thomas Dorsey was straddling his career in popular music and a commitment to compose sacred music when he suffered the loss of his wife and son during childbirth in 1932. He composed "Precious Lord, Take My Hand" while dealing with his grief, launching a pioneering gospel music career that included collaborations with Sallie Martin and Mahalia Jackson.

Precious Lord, take my hand,
Lead me on, let me stand,
I am tired, I am weak, I am worn;
Through the storm, through the night,
Lead me on to the light:

*Refrain:*
*Take my hand, precious Lord,*
*Lead me home.*

When my way grows drear,
Precious Lord, linger near,
When my life is almost gone,
Hear my cry, hear my call,
Hold my hand lest I fall:

*Refrain*

When the darkness appears
And the night draws near,
And the day is past and gone,
At the river I stand,
Guide my feet, hold my hand:

*Refrain*

# SAY IT LOUD—I'M BLACK AND I'M PROUD

*James Brown* — 1968

Soul singer and composer James Brown was involved in a variety of civil rights activities during the late 1960s and early 1970s and his landmark single "Say It Loud" became one of the black power anthems of the period.

*Excerpt:*
Uh, with your bad self!

. . . . . . . . .

Say it loud!—I'm black and I'm proud
Say it louder—I'm black and I'm proud

Now we demand a chance to do things for ourselves
We tired of beatin' our heads against the wall
And workin' for someone else
A-look-a-here
There's one thing more I got to say right here
Now, now we're people, we're like the birds and the bees
We'd rather die on our feet than keep livin' on our knees . . .

# Prose & Poetry

## A VOICE FROM THE SOUTH
## BY A BLACK WOMAN OF THE SOUTH

*Anna Julia Cooper* — *1892*

Born into slavery, Anna Julia Cooper was one of the first black women graduates from Oberlin College, and she earned her doctorate at the Sorbonne at the age of 66. Her book *A Voice from the South* includes speeches and essays expressing her views as a women's rights and political activist.

*Excerpt:*

Now please understand me. I do not ask you to admit that these benefactions and virtues are the exclusive possession of women, or even that women are their chief and only advocates. It may be a man who formulates and makes them vocal. It may be, and often is, a man who weeps over the wrongs and struggles for the amelioration: but that man has imbibed those impulses from a mother rather than from a father and is simply materializing and giving back to the world in tangible form the ideal love and tenderness, devotion and care that have cherished and nourished the helpless period of his own existence.

All I claim is that there is a feminine as well as a masculine side to truth; that these are related not as inferior and superior, not as better and worse, not as weaker and stronger, but as complements—complements in one necessary and symmetric whole. That as the man is more noble in reason, so the woman is more quick in sympathy. That as he is indefatigable in pursuit of abstract truth, so is she in caring for the interests by the way—striving tenderly and lovingly that not one of the least of these "little ones" should perish. That while we not unfrequently [sic] see women who reason, we say, with the coolness and precision of a man, and men as considerate of helplessness as a woman, still there is a general consensus of mankind that the one trait is essentially masculine and the other as peculiarly feminine. That both are needed to be worked into the training of children, in order that our boys may supplement their virility by tenderness and sensibility, and our girls may round out their gentleness by strength and self-reliance. That, as both are alike necessary in giving symmetry to the individual, so a nation or a race will degenerate into mere emotionalism on the one hand, or bullyism on the other, if dominated by either exclusively; lastly, and most emphatically, that the feminine factor can have its proper effect only through woman's development and education so that she may fitly and intelligently stamp her force on the forces of her day, and add her modicum to the riches of the world's thought.

# I, TOO

*Langston Hughes* ⟶ *1924*

Langston Hughes, the most prolific and widely recognized writer emerging from the Harlem Renaissance period, wrote "I, Too" in 1924. As in later works, Hughes struggles with the contradictions between the ideal of being an American and the realities of black life in America.

I, too, sing America.

I am the darker brother.
They send me to eat in the kitchen
When company comes,
But I laugh,
And eat well,
And grow strong.

Tomorrow,
I'll be at the table
When company comes.
Nobody'll dare
Say to me,
"Eat in the kitchen,"
Then.

Besides,
They'll see how beautiful I am
And be ashamed—

I, too, am America.

# AUTOBIOGRAPHICAL NOTES

*James Baldwin* — 1952

This piece became part of James Baldwin's 1955 compilation of essays *Notes of a Native Son*. The book, which established his reputation as one of the most prophetic voices of the twentieth century, was written during a decade spent in France. In 1957, he abandoned his life in exile to become involved in the US civil rights movement.

*Excerpt:*

One of the difficulties about being a Negro writer (and this is not special pleading, since I don't mean to suggest that he has it worse than anybody else) is that the Negro problem is written about so widely. The bookshelves groan under the weight of information, and everyone therefore considers himself informed. And this information, furthermore, operates usually (generally, popularly) to reinforce traditional attitudes. Of traditional attitudes there are only two—For or Against—and I, personally, find it difficult to say which attitude has caused me the most pain. I am speaking as a writer; from a social point of view I am perfectly aware that the change from ill-will to good-will, however motivated, however imperfect, however expressed, is better than no change at all.

But it is part of the business of the writer—as I see it—to examine attitudes, to go beneath the surface, to tap the source. From this point of view the Negro problem is nearly inaccessible. It is not only written about so widely; it is written about so badly. It is quite possible to say that the price a Negro pays for becoming articulate is to find himself, at length, with nothing to be articulate about. ("You taught me language," says Caliban to Prospero, "and my profit on't is I know how to curse.") Consider: the tremendous social activity that this problem generates imposes on whites and Negroes alike the necessity of looking forward, of working to bring about a better day. This is fine, it keeps the waters troubled; it is all, indeed, that has made possible the Negro's progress. Nevertheless, social affairs are not generally speaking the writer's prime concern, whether they ought to be or not; it is absolutely necessary that he establish between himself and these affairs a distance which will allow, at least, for clarity, so that before he can look forward in any meaningful sense, he must first be allowed to take a long look back. In the context of the Negro problem neither whites nor blacks, for excellent reasons of their own, have the faintest desire to look back; but I think that the past is all that makes the present coherent, and further, that the past will remain horrible for exactly as long as we refuse to assess it honestly.

# ON THE PULSE OF MORNING

*Maya Angelou* ⌐ *Presidential Inauguration Ceremony, January 20, 1993*

**Distinguished writer and educator Maya Angelou, who spent part of her childhood years in Arkansas, was chosen by former Arkansas Governor Bill Clinton to deliver the inaugural poem at his first swearing-in ceremony as President of the United States.**

*Excerpt:*
Each of you, descendant of some passed
On traveller, has been paid for.
You, who gave me my first name, you,
Pawnee, Apache, Seneca, you
Cherokee Nation, who rested with me, then
Forced on bloody feet,
Left me to the employment of
Other seekers—desperate for gain,
Starving for gold.
You, the Turk, the Arab, the Swede, the German, the Eskimo, the Scot,
You the Ashanti, the Yoruba, the Kru, bought,
Sold, stolen, arriving on the nightmare
Praying for a dream.
Here, root yourselves beside me.
I am that Tree planted by the River,
Which will not be moved.
I, the Rock, I the River, I the Tree
I am yours—your Passages have been paid.
Lift up your faces, you have a piercing need
For this bright morning dawning for you.
History, despite its wrenching pain
Cannot be unlived, but if faced
With courage, need not be lived again. . . .

# African Americans in Congress

| NAME | YEARS OF SERVICE | STATE & PARTY |
|---|---|---|
| **Senators** | | |
| Revels, Hiram Rhodes* | 1870–71 | MS-R |
| *(\*First black elected to Senate)* | | |
| Bruce, Blanche Kelso | 1875–81 | MS-R |
| Brooke, Edward William, III | 1967–79 | MA-R |
| Moseley Braun, Carol* | 1993–99 | IL-D |
| *(\*First black woman elected to Senate)* | | |
| Obama, Barack* | 2005–2008 | IL-D |
| *(\*Democratic Party's first African-American nominee for U.S. presidency and first African-American U.S. president)* | | |
| **Representatives** | | |
| Rainey, Joseph Hayne* | 1870–79 | SC-R |
| *(\*First black member of House; elected in special election after House declared Benjamin Franklin Whittemore's seat vacant)* | | |
| Long, Jefferson Franklin* | 1870–71 | GA-R |
| *(\*In 1871 delivered the first speech on floor of Congress by a black member)* | | |
| Elliott, Robert Brown | 1871–74 | SC-R |
| DeLarge, Robert Carlos | 1871–73 | SC-R |
| Turner, Benjamin S. | 1871–73 | AL-R |
| Walls, Josiah Thomas | 1871–73, 1873–75, 1875–76 | FL-R |
| Cain, Richard Harvey | 1873–75, 1877–79 | SC-R |
| Lynch, John Roy | 1873–77, 1882–83 | MS-R |
| Ransier, Alonzo Jacob | 1873–75 | SC-R |
| Rapier, James Thomas | 1873–75 | AL-R |
| Haralson, Jeremiah | 1875–77 | AL-R |
| Hyman, John Adams | 1875–77 | NC-R |
| Nash, Charles Edmund | 1875–77 | LA-R |
| Smalls, Robert | 1875–79, 1882–83, 1884–87 | SC-R |
| O'Hara, James Edward | 1883–87 | NC-R |
| Cheatham, Henry Plummer | 1889–93 | NC-R |
| Langston, John Mercer | 1890–91 | VA-R |
| Miller, Thomas Ezekiel | 1890–91 | SC-R |
| Murray, George Washington | 1893–95, 1896–97 | SC-R |
| White, George Henry* | 1897–1901 | NC-R |
| *(\*Only black member of Congress during his tenure; 28 years passed before another black member was seated)* | | |
| DePriest, Oscar Stanton | 1929–35 | IL-R |
| Mitchell, Arthur Wergs* | 1935–43 | IL-D |
| *(\*First black Democrat elected to Congress)* | | |
| Dawson, William Levi | 1943–70 | IL-D |
| Powell, Adam Clayton, Jr. | 1945–67, 1969–71 | NY-D |
| Diggs, Charles Coles, Jr. | 1955–80 | MI-D |
| Nix, Robert Nelson Cornelius, Sr. | 1958–79 | PA-D |
| Hawkins, Augustus Freeman | 1963–91 | CA-D |

| NAME | YEARS OF SERVICE | STATE & PARTY |
|---|---|---|
| Conyers, John, Jr. | 1965– | MI-D |
| (*Principal sponsor of the bill leading to the Martin Luther King Jr.Holiday Act of 1983) | | |
| Chisholm, Shirley Anita** | 1969–83 | NY-D |
| (**First black woman elected to Congress; first black woman to run for president [1972]) | | |
| Clay, William Lacy, Sr. | 1969–2001 | MO-D |
| Stokes, Louis | 1969–99 | OH-D |
| Collins, George Washington | 1970–72 | IL-D |
| Dellums, Ronald Vernie* | 1971–98 | CA-D |
| (*Primary sponsor of legislation that ended US support of apartheid in South Africa) | | |
| Fauntroy, Walter Edward | 1971–91 | DC-D |
| Metcalfe, Ralph Harold | 1971–78 | IL-D |
| Mitchell, Parren James | 1971–87 | MD-D |
| Rangel, Charles Bernard | 1971– | NY-D |
| Burke, Yvonne Brathwaite* | 1973–79 | CA-D |
| (*First woman to give birth while serving in Congress, in 1973) | | |
| Collins, Cardiss | 1973–79 | IL-D |
| Jordan, Barbara Charline | 1973–79 | TX-D |
| Young, Andrew Jackson, Jr.* | 1973–77 | GA-D |
| (*Resigned January 29, 1977, to become US Ambassador to United Nations) | | |
| Ford, Harold Eugene, Sr. | 1975–97 | TN-D |
| Dixon, Julian Carey | 1979–2000 | CA-D |
| Evans, Melvin Herbert | 1979–81 | VI-R |
| Gray, William Herbert, III | 1979–91 | PA-D |
| Leland, George Thomas "Mickey" | 1979–89 | TX-D |
| Stewart, Bennett McVey | 1979–81 | IL-D |
| Crockett, George William, Jr. | 1980–91 | MI-D |
| Dymally, Mervyn Malcolm | 1981–93 | CA-D |
| Savage, Gus | 1981–93 | IL-D |
| Washington, Harold D. | 1981–83 | IL-D |
| Hall, Katie Beatrice | 1982–85 | IN-D |
| Hayes, Charles Arthur | 1983–93 | IL-D |
| Owens, Major Robert Odell | 1983–2007 | NY-D |
| Towns, Edolphus | 1983– | NY-D |
| Wheat, Alan Dupree | 1983–95 | MO-D |
| Waldon, Alton R., Jr. | 1986–87 | NY-D |
| Espy, Alphonso Michael "Mike"* | 1987–93 | MS-D |
| (*Resigned January 25, 1993, to become Secretary of Agriculture) | | |
| Flake, Floyd Harold | 1987–97 | NY-D |
| Lewis, John R. | 1987– | GA-D |
| Mfume, Kweisi | 1987–96 | MD-D |
| Payne, Donald Milford | 1989– | NJ-D |
| Washington, Craig Anthony | 1989–95 | TX-D |
| Blackwell, Lucien Edward | 1991–95 | PA-D |
| Collins, Barbara-Rose | 1991–97 | MI-D |
| Franks, Gary A. | 1991–97 | CT-R |
| Jefferson, William Jennings | 1991– | LA-D |
| Norton, Eleanor Holmes | 1991– | DC-D |

| NAME | YEARS OF SERVICE | STATE & PARTY |
|------|------------------|---------------|
| Waters, Maxine | 1991– | CA-D |
| Clayton, Eva M. | 1992–2003 | NC-D |
| Bishop, Sanford Dixon, Jr. | 1993– | GA-D |
| Brown, Corrine | 1993– | FL-D |
| Clyburn, James Enos | 1993– | SC-D |
| Fields, Cleo | 1993–97 | LA-D |
| Hastings, Alcee Lamar | 1993– | FL-D |
| Hilliard, Earl Frederick | 1993–2003 | AL-D |
| Johnson, Eddie Bernice | 1993– | TX-D |
| McKinney, Cynthia Ann | 1993–2003, 2005–7 | GA-D |
| Meek, Carrie P. | 1993–2003 | FL-D |
| Reynolds, Mel J. | 1993–95 | IL-D |
| Rush, Bobby L. | 1993– | IL-D |
| Scott, Robert Cortez | 1993– | VA-D |
| Thompson, Bennie G. | 1993– | MS-D |
| Tucker, Walter R., III | 1993–95 | CA-D |
| Watt, Melvin L. | 1993– | NC-D |
| Wynn, Albert Russell | 1993–2008 | MD-D |
| Fattah, Chaka | 1995– | PA-D |
| Frazer, Victor O. | 1995–97 | VI-I |
| Jackson, Jesse L., Jr. | 1995– | IL-D |
| Jackson-Lee, Sheila | 1995– | TX-D |
| Watts, Julius Caesar "J. C.," Jr. | 1995–2003 | OK-R |
| Cummings, Elijah E. | 1996– | MD-D |
| Millender-McDonald, Juanita | 1996–2007 | CA-D |
| Ford, Harold Eugene, Jr. | 1997–2007 | TN-D |
| Kilpatrick, Carolyn Cheeks | 1997– | MI-D |
| Carson, Julia | 1997–2007 | IN-D |
| Christensen, Donna Marie Christian | 1997– | VI-D |
| Davis, Danny K. | 1997– | IL-D |
| Lee, Barbara | 1998– | CA-D |
| Meeks, Gregory W. | 1998– | NY-D |
| Jones, Stephanie Tubbs | 1999– | OH-D |
| Clay, William Lacy, Jr. | 2001– | MO-D |
| Watson, Diane Edith | 2001– | CA-D |
| Ballance, Frank W., Jr. | 2003–4 | NC-D |
| Davis, Artur | 2003– | AL-D |
| Majette, Denise L. | 2003–5 | GA-D |
| Meek, Kendrick B. | 2003– | FL-D |
| Scott, David | 2003– | GA-D |
| Butterfield, George Kenneth "G. K.," Jr. | 2003– | NC-D |
| Cleaver, Emanuel, II | 2005– | MO-D |
| Green, Al | 2005– | TX-D |
| Moore, Gwendolynne "Gwen" S. | 2005– | WI-D |
| Ellison, Keith | 2007– | MN-D |
| Clarke, Yvette Diane | 2007– | NY-D |
| Johnson, Hank | 2007– | GA-D |
| Richardson, Laura | 2007– | CA-D |

Note: Listed district does not include all districts a member may have represented.
Sources: MS Encarta; Congressional Research Service, Black Members of the United States Congress: 1789–1997 and Black Members of the United States Congress: 1870–2004.

An etching from *Frank Leslie's Illustrated Newspaper* of the Colored Convention in Nashville, Tennessee, 1876.

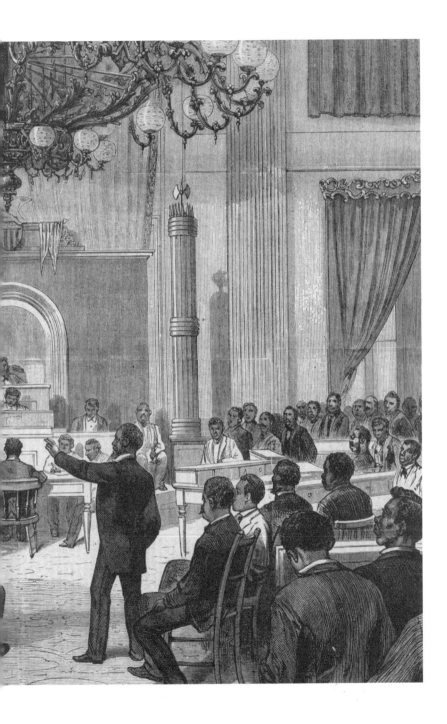

# African & African Diasporan Populations

| Sub-Saharan Africa | 750,000,000 |
|---|---|
| Western Africa | 283,000,000 |
| Eastern Africa | 294,000,000 |
| Central Africa | 118,000,000 |
| Southern Africa | 55,000,000 |

| Central and South America | 102,440,000 |
|---|---|
| Argentina | * |
| Belize | 93,000 |
| Bolivia | 108,000 |
| Brazil | 85,783,000 |
| Chile | * |
| Colombia | 9,453,000 |
| Costa Rica | 130,000 |
| Ecuador | 418,000 |
| French Guiana | 133,000 |
| Guyana | 278,000 |
| Honduras | 153,000 |
| Mexico | 1,100,000 |
| Nicaragua | 521,000 |
| Panama | 461,000 |
| Paraguay | * |
| Peru | 875,000 |
| Surinam | 195,000 |
| Uruguay | 139,000 |
| Venezuela | 2,600,000 |

| | |
|---|---|
| *Caribbean* | *27,830,000* |
| Anguilla | 14,000 |
| Antigua and Barbuda | 70,000 |
| Bahamas | 307,000 |
| Barbados | 282,000 |
| Bermuda | 67,000 |
| British Virgin Islands | 24,000 |
| Cayman Islands | 48,000 |
| Cuba | 3,998,000 |
| Dominica | 73,000 |
| Dominican Republic | 7,986,000 |
| El Salvador | * |
| Grenada | 90,000 |
| Guadeloupe | 436,000 |
| Guatemala | 260,000 |
| Haiti | 8,925,000 |
| Jamaica | 2,804,000 |
| Martinique | 401,000 |
| Netherlands Antilles | 225,000 |
| Puerto Rico | 752,000 |
| St. Kitts and Nevis | 40,000 |
| St. Lucia | 173,000 |
| St. Vincent and the Grenadines | 118,000 |
| Trinidad and Tobago | 607,000 |
| Turks and Caicos Islands | 22,000 |
| U.S. Virgin Islands | 108,000 |

| | |
|---|---|
| *North America* | |
| Canada | 830,000 |
| United States | 44,055,000 |

| | |
|---|---|
| **Total in the Americas** | 173,815,000 |

---

\* N/A, below 1%.

Sources: Figures for Africa were compiled from Population Reference Bureau, 2007 estimates;
figures for the Americas from The World Factbook, Central Intelligence Agency, estimates for 2008.

# Bibliography

Appiah, Anthony, and Henry L. Gates. *Africana: The Encyclopedia of the African and African American Experience*. New York: Oxford University Press, 2005.

Aptheker, Herbert. *A Documentary History of the Negro People in the United States*. New York: Citadel Press, 1969.

Atmore, A. E. "From Angola to Mozambique: Portuguese Economic Activities and their Outreach." *Cambridge History of Africa* 6 (1985): 78.

Bethune, Mary M. "The Sacrifices and Achievements of African-American Women." *The Journal of Blacks in Higher Education* 32 (2001): 35.

"Biographical Data: Guion S. Bluford, Jr. (Colonel, USAF, Ret.)." NASA. 2008 http://www.jsc.nasa.gov/Bios/htmlbios/bluford-gs.html.

Blackburn, Robin. *The Making of New World Slavery: From the Baroque to the Modern, 1492–1800*. London: Verso, 1997.

Blakely, Allison. *Blacks in the Dutch World: The Evolution of Racial Imagery in a Modern Society*. Bloomington: Indiana University Press, 1993.

Borio, Gene. "The Tobacco Timeline." Tobacco.Org. 2007. http://www.tobacco.org/History/Tobacco_History.html.

Bowser, Frederick P. *The African Slave in Colonial Peru, 1524–1650*. Stanford, CA: Stanford University Press, 1974.

Bugner, Ladislas. *The Image of the Black in Western Art, Volume II*. New York: William Morrow, 1976.

Burrows, Edwin G., and Mike Wallace. *Gotham: A History of New York City to 1898*. New York: Oxford University Press, 1999.

"Call to the Third Congress of Black Culture in the Americas (São Paulo, Brazil, August 1982)." *Journal of Black Studies* 12.2 (1981): 123–125.

Carson, Clayborne, et al. *Civil Rights Chronicle: The African-American Struggle for Freedom*. Lincolnwood, IL: Legacy, 2003.

Chapelle, Tony. "Adam Clayton Powell, Jr.: Black Power Between Heaven and Hell." *Black Collegian*. [2003?] http://www.black-collegian.com/african/adam.shtml.

Chappell, Kevin. "Jesse Jackson's Wall Street Initiative." *Ebony*, February 1999.

Christian, Charles M., and Sari Bennett. *Black Saga: The African American Experience. A Chronology*. New York: Civitas/Counterpoint, 1999.

Clarke, J. D. *The Cambridge History of Africa: Vol. 1, From the Earliest Times to c. 500 BC*. Cambridge: Cambridge University Press, 1982.

"Clashes in Illinois Bring Out Troops." *New York Times*, July 13, 1951.

Cook, Noble D. *Born to Die: Disease and New World Conquest, 1492–1650*. Cambridge: Cambridge University Press, 1998.

"Cotton manufacturing exports in England surpass wool." *Times of London*. October 31, 1811: 3. [Digital Archives, New York Public Library]

Curtin, Philip D. *The Atlantic Slave Trade: A Census*. Madison: University of Wisconsin Press, 1969.

Dodson, Howard. *Jubilee: The Emergence of African-American Culture*. Washington, DC: National Geographic Books, 2000.

Dodson, Howard, and Sylviane Diouf. *In Motion: The African-American Migration Experience*. Washington, DC: National Geographic Society, 2004.

Dunn, Richard S. *Sugar and Slaves: The Rise of the Planter Class in the English West Indies, 1624–1713*. London: W. W. Norton & Company, 1973.

*Encyclopedia of African-American Culture and History*. 2nd edition. 6 vols. Editor in Chief, Colin Palmer. Detroit: MacMillan Reference USA in association with The Schomburg Center for Research in Black Culture, 2006.

*Encyclopedia Britannica*. 15th edition. Chicago: Encyclopedia Britannica, Inc., 1986.

Etlin, Richard A. *Art, Culture, and Media Under the Third Reich*. Chicago: University of Chicago Press, 2002.

Finkelman, Paul. *Slave Trade and Migration: Domestic and Foreign*. New York: Garland Publishing, 1989.

Garvin, Glenn. "The African Americans of D-Day." *Miami Herald*. February 2007. Military.com http://www.military.com/NewsContent/0,13319,126337,00.html.

Gates, Henry L., and Maria Wolff. "An Overview of Sources on the Life and Work of Juan Latino, the 'Ethiopian Humanist.'" *Research in African Literatures* 29.4 (1998): 14–51.

Hamilton, Charles V. *Adam Clayton Powell, Jr.: The Political Biography of an American Dilemma*. New York: Cooper Square Press, 2002.

Higginbotham, A. Leon. *In the Matter of Color: Race and the American Legal Process—The Colonial Period*. New York: Oxford University Press, 1978.

"In Genial Mood." *Boston Daily Globe.* November 6, 1905.

Jenkins, Everett. *Pan-African Chronology: A Comprehensive Reference to the Black Quest for Freedom in Africa, the Americas, Europe, and Asia.* Jefferson, NC: McFarland, 1996.

Jenkins, Everett. *Pan-African Chronology II: A Comprehensive Reference to the Black Quest for Freedom in Africa, the Americas, Europe, and Asia, 1865–1915.* Jefferson, NC: McFarland, 1998.

Kazal, Russell A. "Making Americans: Immigration, Race, and the Origins of the Diverse Democracy." *Journal of Interdisciplinary History* 33.1 (2002): 142–144.

Kitching, Paula. *Scotland and the Slave Trade: 2007 Bicentenary of the Slave Trade Act.* Edinburgh: Scottish Executive, 2007.

"Letters of Wouter van Twiller and the Director General and Council of New Netherland to the Amsterdam Chamber of the Dutch West India Company, August 14, 1636." *Quarterly Journal of the New York State Historical Association* 1 (1919): 44–50.

Lovejoy, Paul E. *Transformations in Slavery: A History of Slavery in Africa.* Cambridge: Cambridge University Press, 2000.

Menzies, Gavin. *1421: The Year China Discovered America.* New York: William Morrow, 2003.

Miller, Kelly. "The Historic Background of the Negro Physician." *The Journal of Negro History* 1.2 (1916): 99–109.

Moore, Christopher P. *Fighting for America: Black Soldiers, The Unsung Heroes of World War II.* New York: Ballantine Books, 2006.

*MSN Encarta.* http://encarta.msn.com.

"A New Native King." *New York Times.* April 30, 1885.

Palmer, Colin A. *The First Passage: Blacks in the Americas 1502–1617.* New York: Oxford University Press, 1995.

Pershing, John J. *My Experiences in the World War.* New York: Frederick Stokes Company, 1931.

Phillips, Ulrich B. *American Negro Slavery: A Survey of the Supply, Employment, and Control of Negro Labor as Determined by the Plantation Régime.* New York: D. Appleton and Co., 1918.

Rampersad, Arnold. *The Life of Langston Hughes, Vol. 1, 1902–1941, I, Too, Sing America.* New York: Oxford University Press, 1986.

Schomburg Center for Research in Black Culture. *African American Desk Reference*. New York: Wiley, 1999.

"Selected Virginia Statutes relating to Slavery." Virtual Jamestown. 1998. http://www.virtualjamestown.org/slavelink.html.

"Slavery and the Making of America." PBS.org. 2004 http://www.pbs.org/wnet/slavery/timeline/1787.html.

Smith, Jessie C. *Black Firsts: 4,000 Ground-breaking and Pioneering Historical Events*. Detroit: Visible Ink, 2003.

Sweet, James H. *Recreating Africa: Culture, Kinship, and Religion in the African-Portuguese World, 1441–1770*. Chapel Hill: University of North Carolina Press, 2003.

"Table 1. United States—Race and Hispanic Origin: 1790 to 1990." U.S. Census Bureau. 2002. http://www.census.gov/population/www/documentation/twps0056.html.

Thomas, Hugh. *The Slave Trade: The Story of the Atlantic Slave Trade, 1440–1870*. New York: Simon & Schuster, 1999.

Weber, Max. *The Protestant Ethic and the Spirit of Capitalism*. Translated by Talcott Parsons. New York: Scribner, 1958.

"Williams the Conqueror: The Legacy of Architect Paul Revere Williams; Ninth Annual Trojans of Ebony Hue Black History Exhibition." *USC Events Calendar. 2004*. University of Southern California. http://www.usc.edu/calendar/events/20489.html.

# Picture Credits and Permissions

## TEXT CREDITS

*page 112:* Speech excerpt of "I Have a Dream" by Martin Luther King Jr.: Reprinted by arrangement with the Heirs to the Estate of Martin Luther King Jr., <sup>c</sup>/o Writers House as agent for the proprietor, New York, NY. Copyright 1963 Martin Luther King Jr., copyright renewed 1991 Coretta Scott King.

*page 114:* Speech excerpt of "The Ballot or the Bullet" by Malcolm X: Printed with permission of the Estate of Malcolm X. All Rights Reserved.

*page 122:* Lyric excerpt of "Say It Loud" by James Brown, 1968. Reprinted with permission of the Estate of James Brown.

*page 124:* "I, Too," from *The Collected Poems of Langston Hughes* by Langston Hughes, edited by Arnold Rampersad with David Roessel, Associate Editor. Copyright © 1994 by The Estate of Langston Hughes. Used by permission of Alfred A. Knopf, a division of Random House, Inc.

*page 125:* From *Notes of a Native Son* by James Baldwin. Copyright © 1955, renewed 1983, by James Baldwin. Reprinted by permission of Beacon Press, Boston.

*page 126:* From "On the Pulse of Morning," by Maya Angelou, copyright © 1983 by Maya Angelou. Used by permission of Random House, Inc.

## PICTURE CREDITS

*Courtesy of Prints & Photographs Division, Library of Congress:* page iv, LC-DIG-pga-02595; page 96, LC-DIG-pga-02130; page 113, LC-DIG-ppmsca-03130; page 115, LC-USZC2-5831.

*Courtesy of Photographs and Prints, Schomburg Center for Research in Black Culture, The New York Public Library:* page ii; page 99; page 104, Robert Weaver Collection; page 108; page 110; page 119; page 130–131.

*Courtesy of the Music Division, Library of Congress:* page 116, M2.3.U6A44.